Music Theory for Singers

Level One

Second Edition

Sarah Sandvig

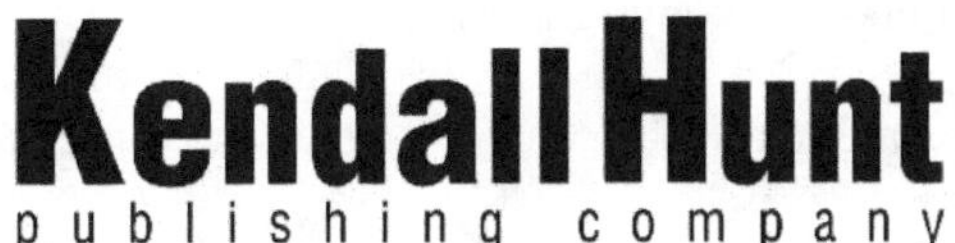

Cover image © Shutterstock, Inc. Used under license.
Back cover image and all keyboard images provided
by the author.

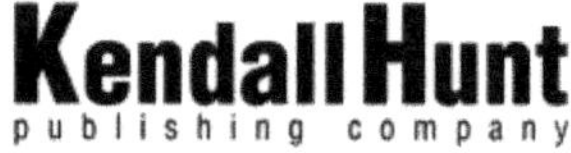

www.kendallhunt.com
Send all inquiries to:
4050 Westmark Drive
Dubuque, IA 52004-1840

ISBN 978-1-5249-1436-3

Published in the United States of America

FOREWORD

In Sarah Sandvig's *Music Theory for Singers*, voice students and their teachers finally have a singer-friendly primer for musicianship and music theory that is directly applicable to voice training. Mrs. Sandvig has capitalized on her experience as a successful private voice teacher to create this comprehensive workbook, which, in clear, concise language, lays out an easy-to-follow lesson plan progressing from basic through advanced skills. *Music Theory for Singers* is equally applicable in a college or high school classroom setting as in the private studio, and voice teachers will especially appreciate the inclusion of international musical terminology, and music history which their students are likely to encounter in vocal repertoire. For teens studying voice for the first time, as well as for life-long adult singers, *Music Theory for Singers* will become a valued adjunct to any level of vocal study.

Juliana Gondek
Metropolitan Opera soloist and
Prize-winning international recording artist
Professor and Chair, Division of Voice Studies
UCLA

I am beginning my first semester as a BFA Musical Theatre Major at The Boston Conservatory at Berklee. I used Sarah's theory books throughout high school from levels 5 through 10, and they have prepared me immensely for this first semester – and beyond. For example, I recently went through a music theory and sight singing placement test: I was so amazed how comfortable I felt with both the written and singing portions. It was everything I had already learned from these theory books – key signatures, scales, rhythm, solfege, and more. In addition, I became so familiar with the fundamentals of music and a piano keyboard (even through utilizing the vocal theory books) I was able to test out of a whole year of beginner piano. All of this creates the possibility for me to move on to higher levels and be more challenged than if I had to start from the basics. Not to mention all of the composers and terms that are necessary knowledge to be successful in professional music classes and settings. It feels good to know that if I am ever unsure about what I am learning in class, my theory books are right there on the bookshelf to help me out.

Sofia Ross
Musical Theatre Major
Boston Conservatory

Thank you to the following people for their help and guidance in writing these books: Mary Beard, Melissa Caldretti, Sally Curry, Sharlae Jenkins, Vanessa Parvin, Connie Venti & my dad, Ken Watson.

Thank you to my husband Darren and sons Aiden & Caleb for their love, support and patience throughout this writing process.

NOTE TO TEACHER:
These books are a supplement to private, group or classroom voice lessons, and though I feel they can stand alone, they are not meant as a replacement for a good teacher who ensures student learning and understanding of music theory, history, and sight-singing. Each book includes reviews of subjects with a review test (with answers) at the end. You may also purchase the Answer Key, which has answers to all pages in each level, 1-10. Composers, terms, IPA and solfege are unique elements of these books that make them especially helpful for singers.

I hope these books are a useful addition to the many tools you already utilize to teach young singers in your studio or classroom.

TABLE OF CONTENTS

MUSIC THEORY FOR SINGERS

LEVEL 1

Lesson 1: Introduction to Beginning Music Theory

If you are new to music instruction, this section will help you understand the basic structure of music, and how it relates to singers.

In music, notes sit on a Staff which consists of 5 lines and 4 spaces. Notes can move up (higher), down (lower), repeat, step or skip. Look at the examples below.

Staff

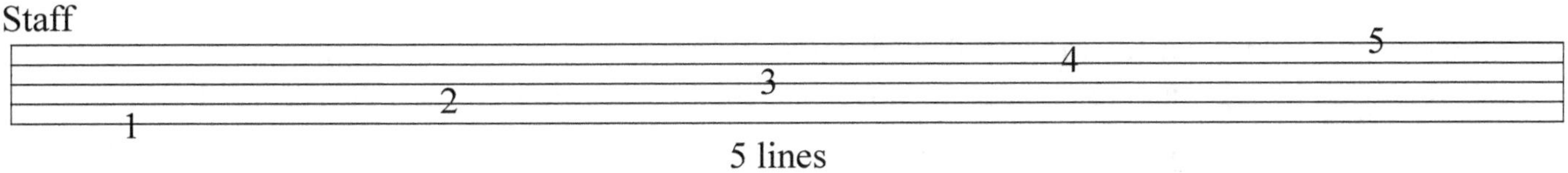

1 2 3 4 5

5 lines

Staff

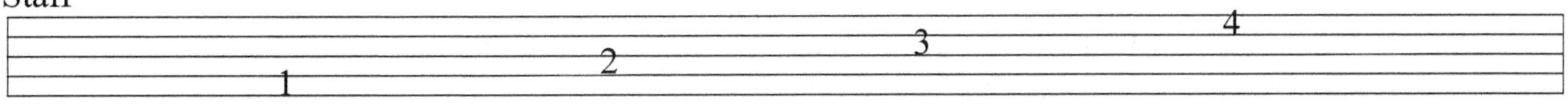

1 2 3 4

4 Spaces

Here is what the notes look like that sit on the lines.

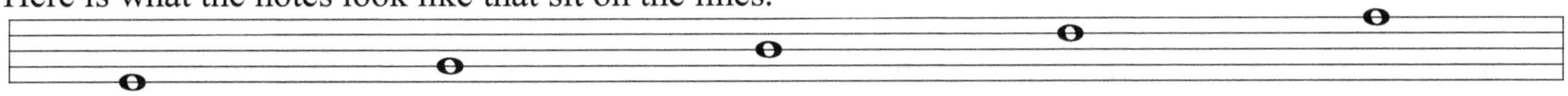

Here is what the notes look like that sit on the spaces.

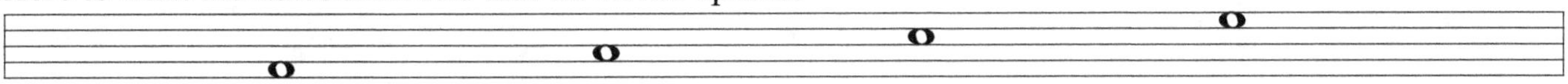

Notes move on the staff in a variety of ways. They move up or down, step or skip or repeat.

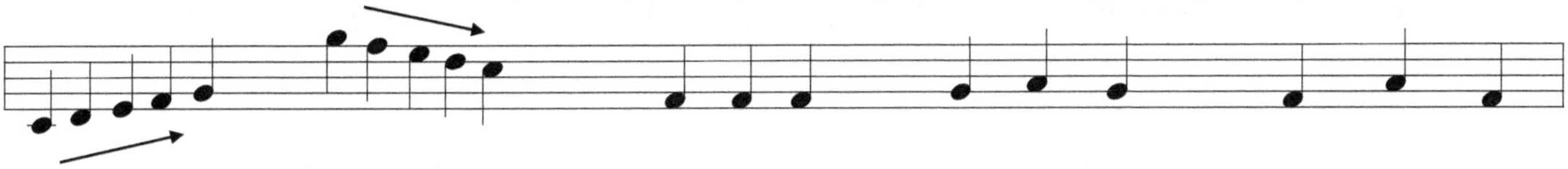

Moving up Moving down Repeating Stepping Skipping

When the notes move higher, your voice gets higher. When the notes move lower, your voice gets lower, and so on. Your voice moves with the notes.

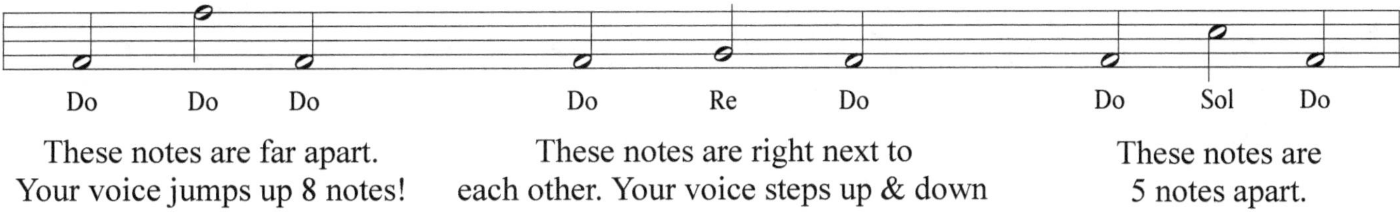

These notes are far apart. Your voice jumps up 8 notes!

These notes are right next to each other. Your voice steps up & down

These notes are 5 notes apart.

Review: Lesson 1

Practice time! Make sure you have a sharp pencil ready!

1. For the following example, write an L for every lined note and an S for every spaced note. The first one is done for you.

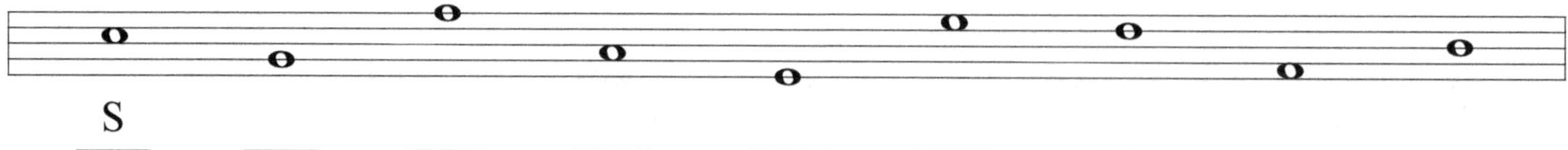

2. Draw ten notes (total) on any of the 5 lines of the staff below. Use whole notes (they look like circles) that were used in the example on page 1. Make sure the line is going through the center of your notes.

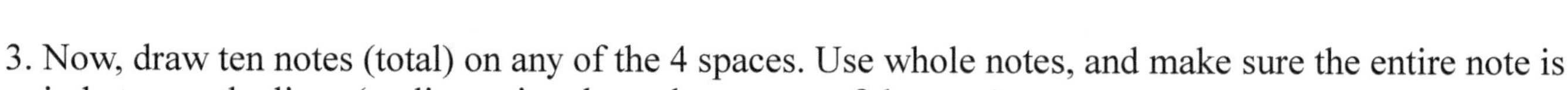

3. Now, draw ten notes (total) on any of the 4 spaces. Use whole notes, and make sure the entire note is in between the lines (no line going through any part of the note).

4. For the examples below, choose whether the notes are moving "Up," "Down" or "Repeating." Remember to look at the note head (circle) not the stem (line connected to notes) to see what direction the notes are moving in. Circle your answer.

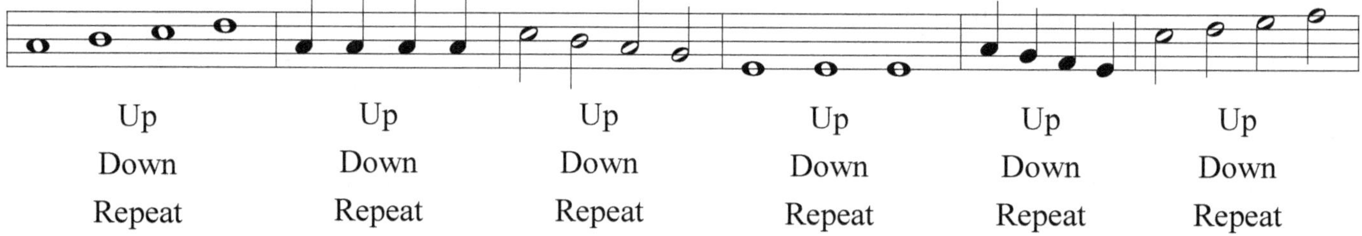

5. Circle "Step" or "Skip" for each example below.

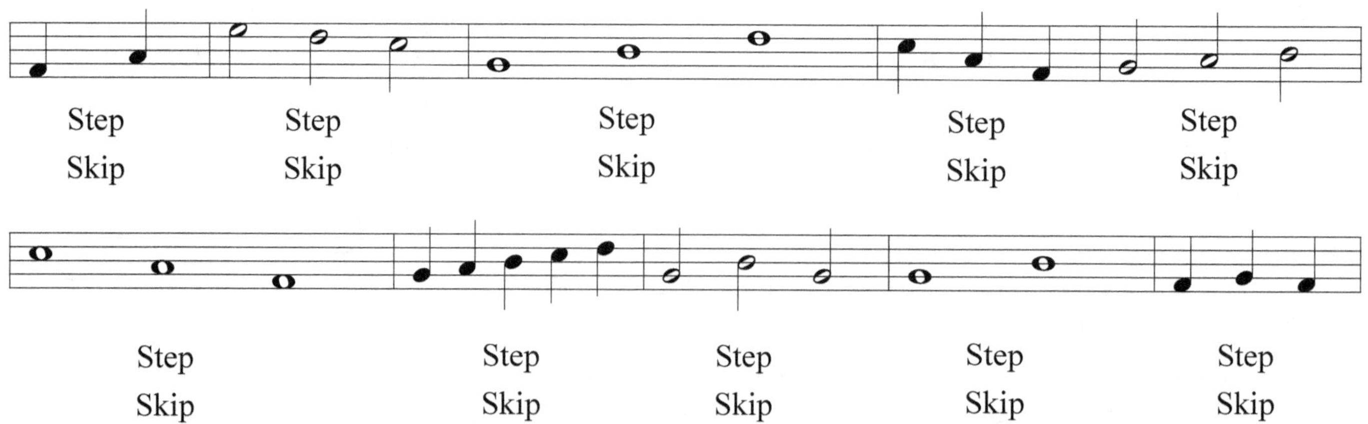

Lesson 2: Singing on the Staff

The melody line for singers is often written on its own staff, with the piano accompaniment below. Look at the example of the vocal warm-up below. The vocal line is using solfege* syllables.

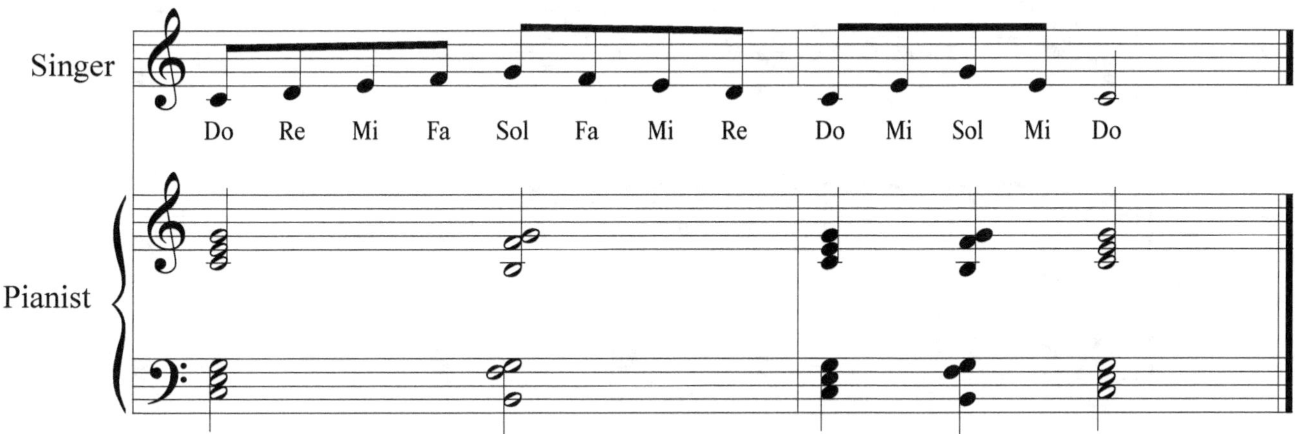

*The Solfege system assigns a syllable to each note of a scale starting with Do. The syllables used for a major scale are: Do Re Mi Fa Sol La Ti Do. Solfege has been in existence for more than 1,000 years!

Other times, the melody for a singer is written into the piano accompaniment. The example below is the same vocal warm-up, but without the separate vocal line. The pianist is now playing the melody with the singer.

Singer sings top line

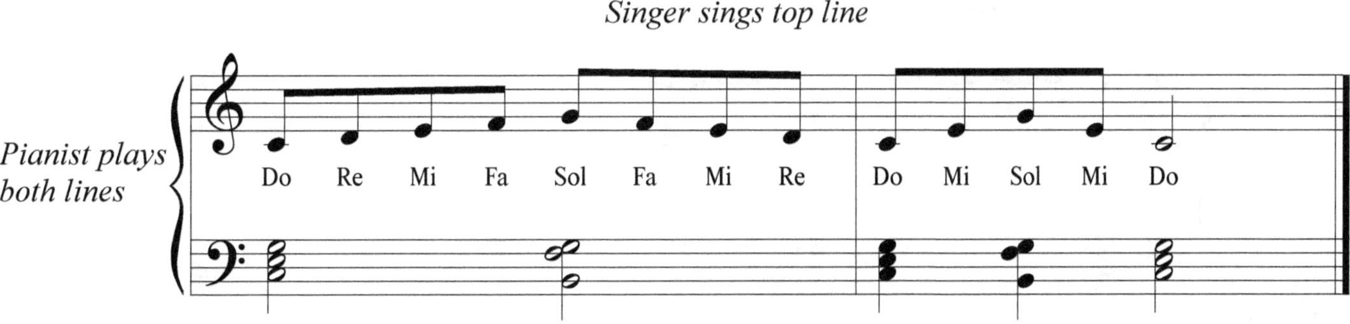

Chord charts are another form of notation where the vocal line (melody) is written out on the staff, and a chord symbol is written above the melody. The alphabet letters indicate what chord(s) (notes) the pianist plays while the singer sings the melody. Guitar or Ukulele tablature may be written above the melody as well.

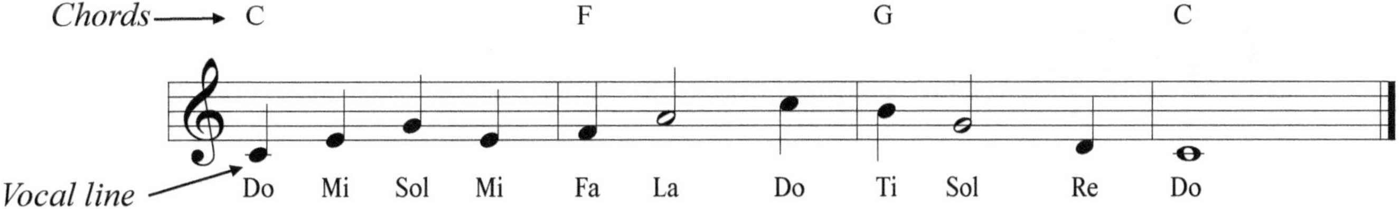

Notes that are on the Treble clef staff are the high notes. The Treble clef (also called the G clef) shows us where the note G is located on the staff.
Female voices (Sopranos, Altos) and sometimes tenor parts are written on a treble clef staff.

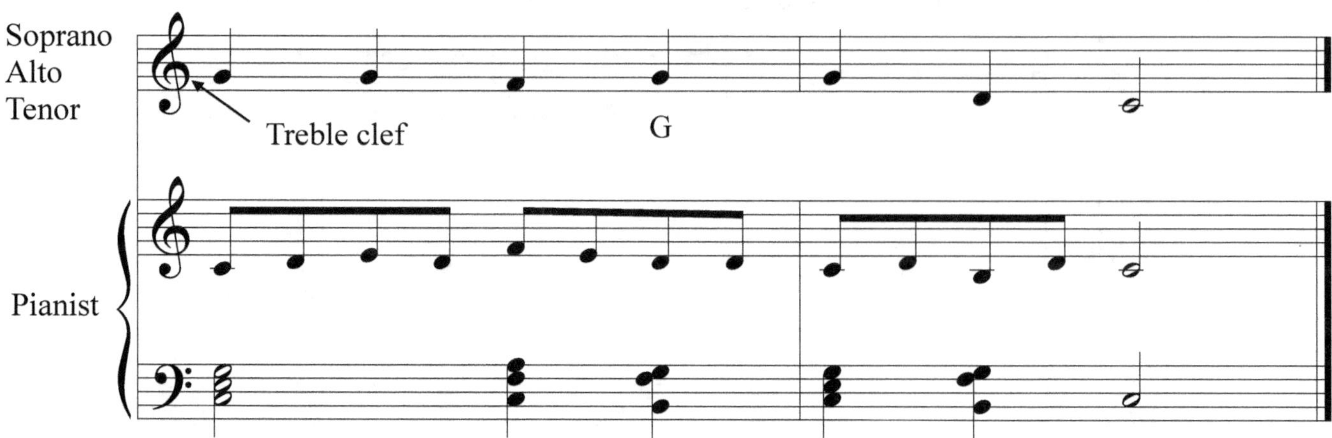

Notes that are on the Bass clef staff are the low notes. The Bass clef (also called the F clef) shows us where the note F is located on the staff.
Male voices (Bass, Baritones, Tenors) are written on a bass clef staff. *

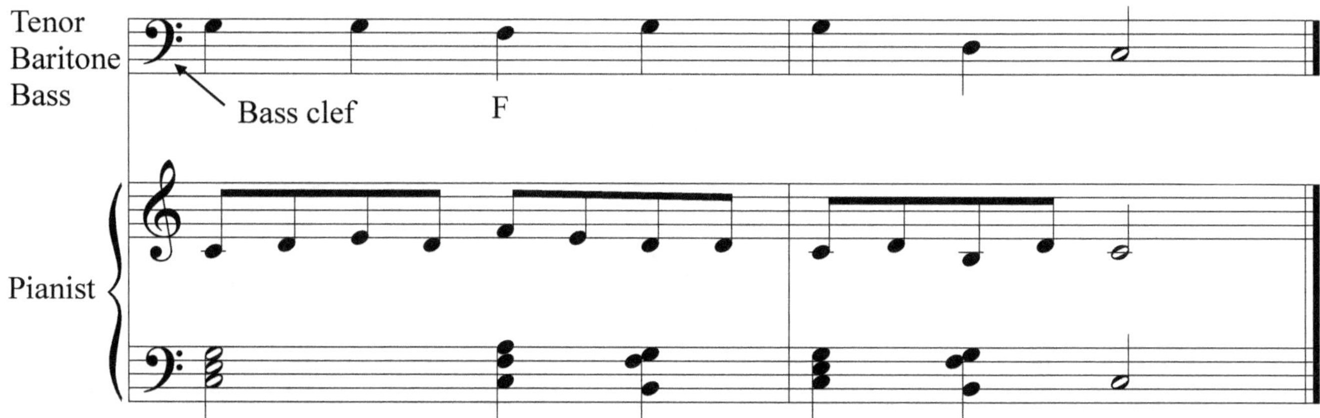

In Choral music, each voice can be written on its own staff, or as in the example below, the higher voices can be written together on the Treble staff and the lower voices can be written together on the Bass staff.

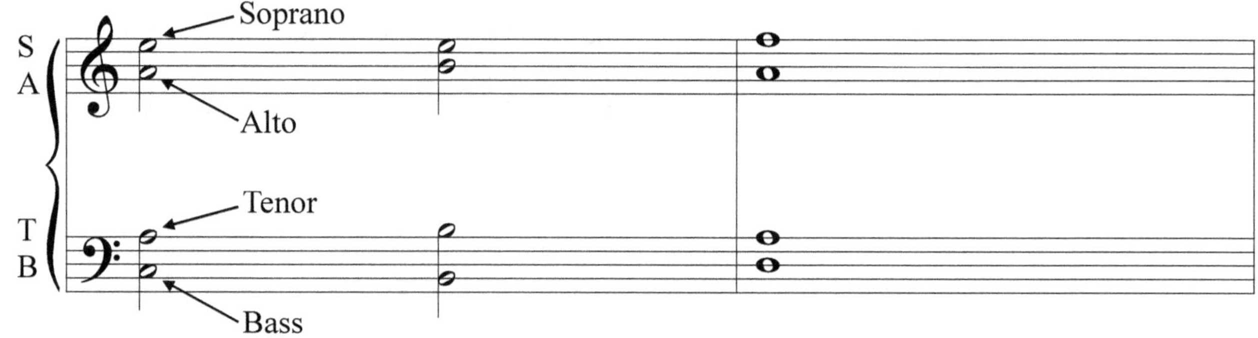

*In Sight-singing exercises, often times examples are written on one staff, usually in the Treble clef, even for male voices.

Review: Lesson 2

Choose the correct term for each of the examples below. Use the following terms:

Choral Music, Chord Chart, Treble clef (High Voices), Piano Accompaniment, Vocal Line, Bass clef (Low Voices)

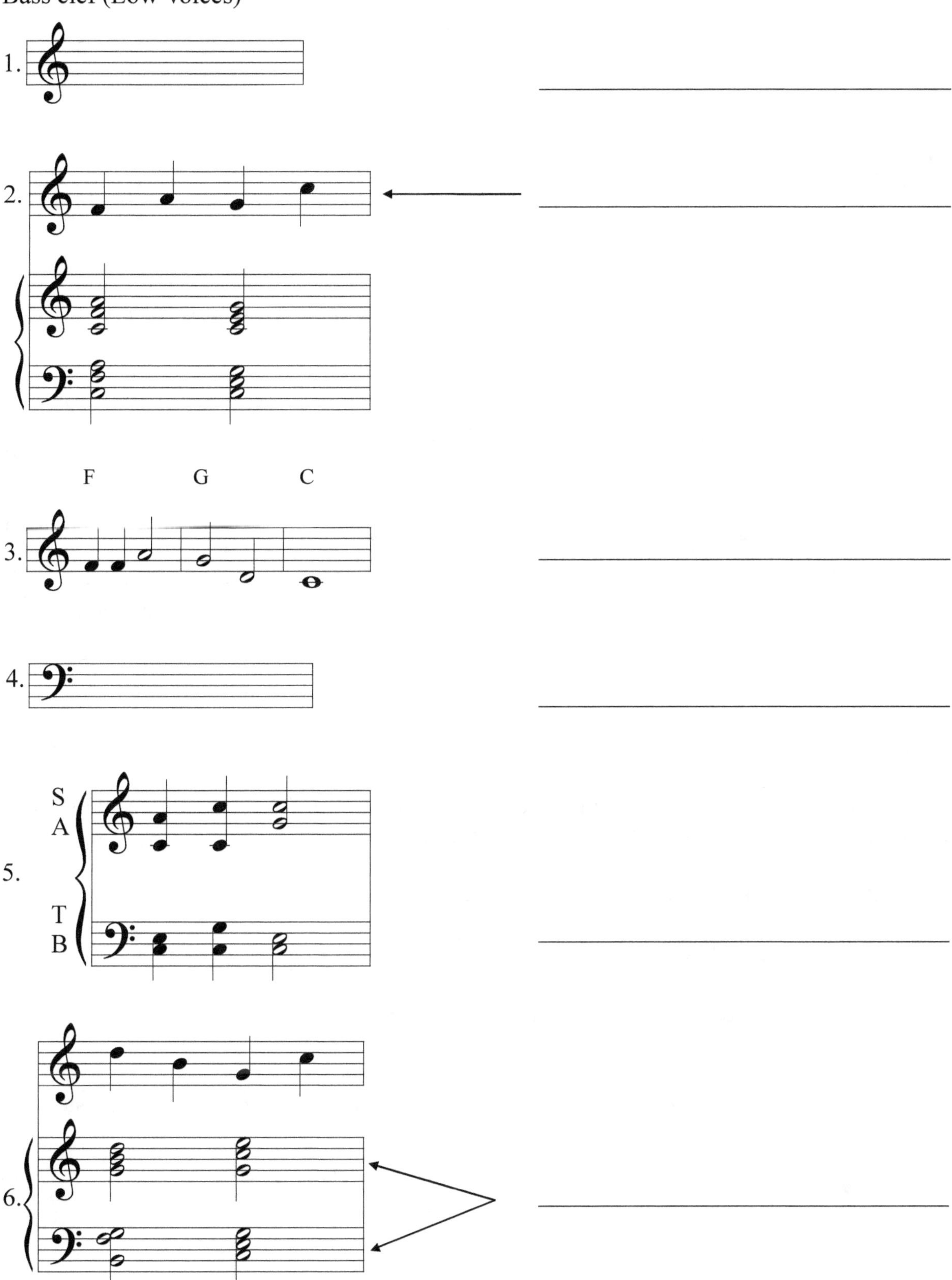

Lesson 3: The Grand Staff

When the treble and bass staves* are joined together by a Brace, it's called a Grand Staff. Pianists (vocal accompanists) play music on a Grand Staff.

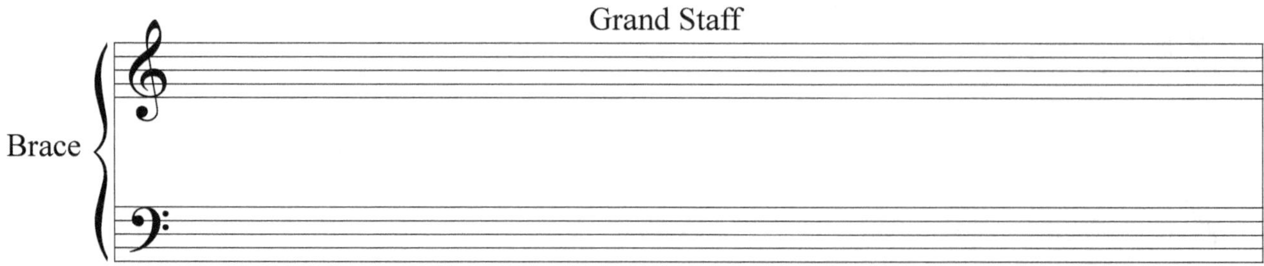

The staff is divided into Measures by Bar Lines. Each measure has the same amount of beats. A Double Bar Line is used to indicate the end of a song or section.

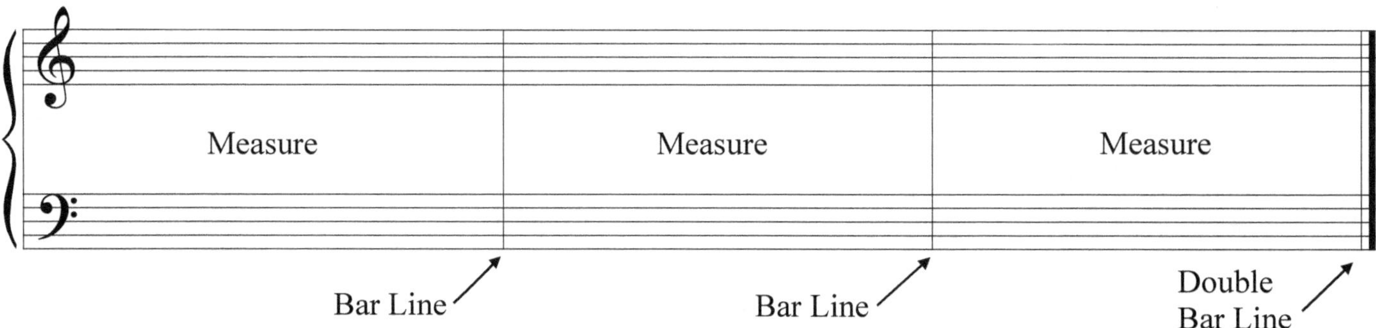

Stem Direction

Most note heads have a stem attached to them, just like the stem of a flower. The only note type that does not have a stem is a whole note (the note that looks like a circle).

- If the note head is above the middle line, the stem goes down on the left.
- If the note head is below the middle line, the stem goes up on the right.
- Note heads on the middle line can have stems going either up or down.

Notes, therefore either look like the lowercase letter "d" or "p" depending on the direction of the stem.

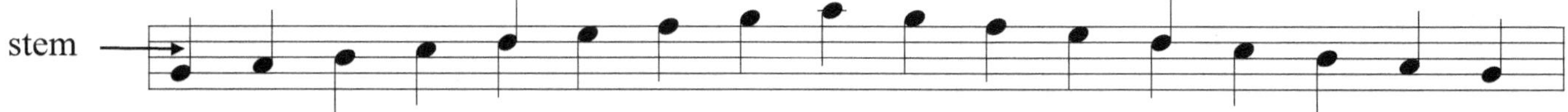

*staves = more than one staff

Review: Lesson 3

1. Look at the musical example below and fill in the appropriate letter next to the term.

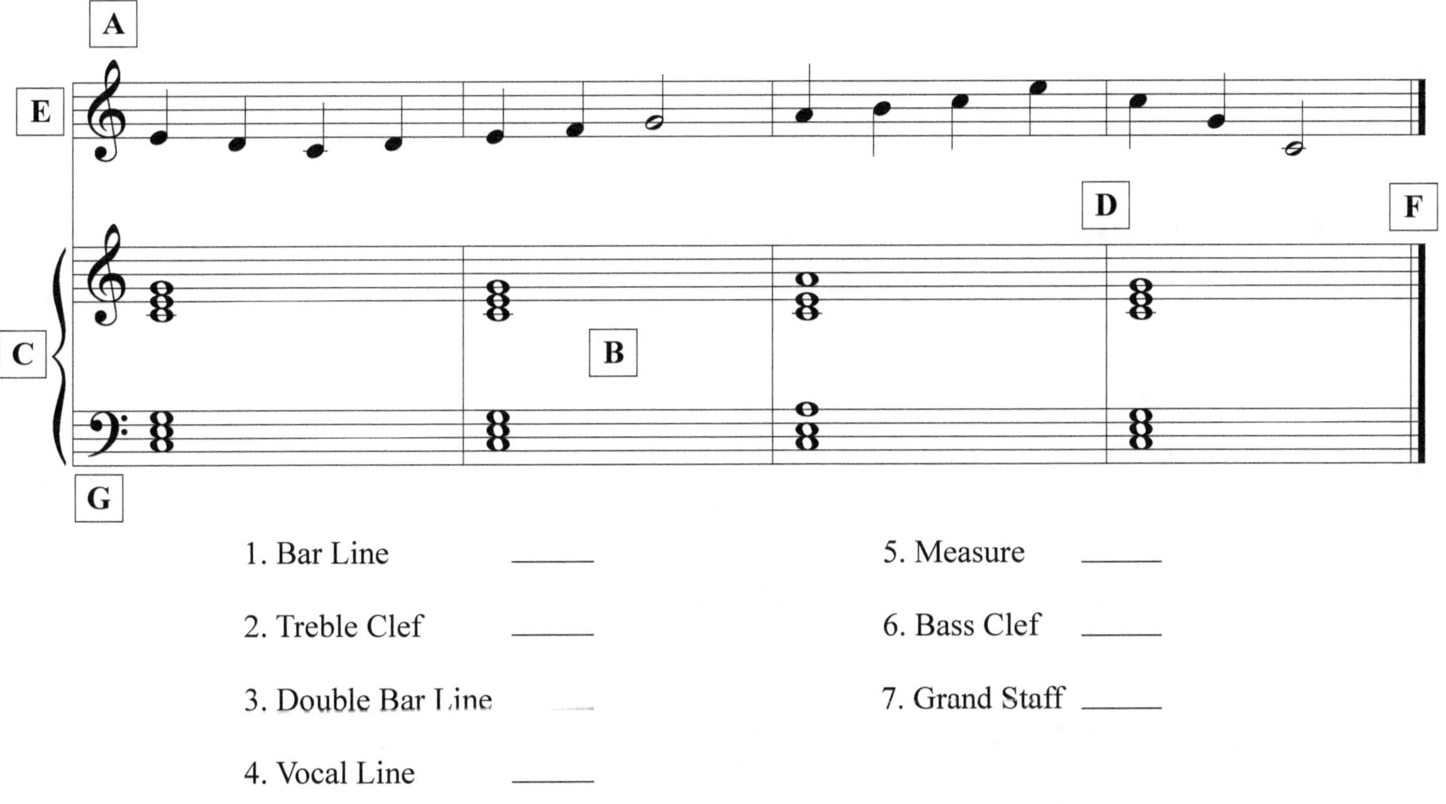

1. Bar Line ______

2. Treble Clef ______

3. Double Bar Line ______

4. Vocal Line ______

5. Measure ______

6. Bass Clef ______

7. Grand Staff ______

2. Let's practice drawing the Treble clef. This can be "trouble" to draw, so look at the steps below. Make sure the inside circle curves around the G line (2nd line from the bottom).

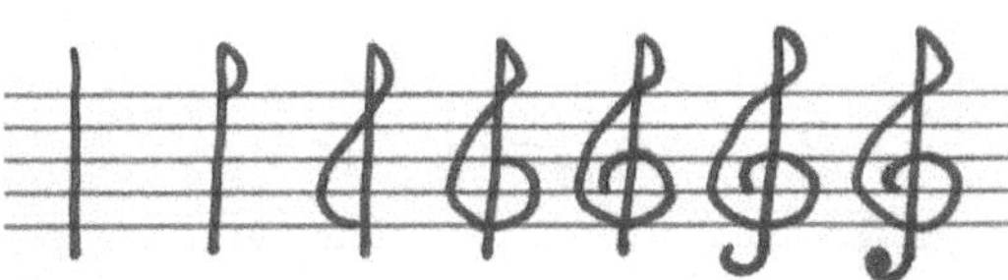

Draw 10 Treble clefs on the blank staff below.

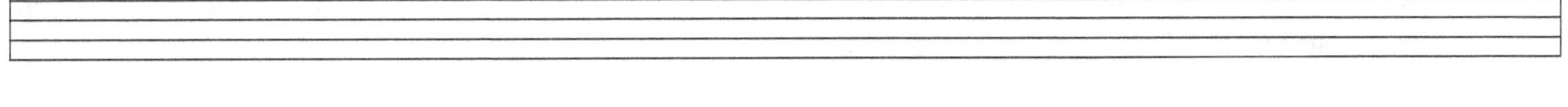

3. Now, let's draw the Bass clef. Make sure the big dot is on the F line (2nd one down from the top), and the two dots after the clef are above and below the F line.

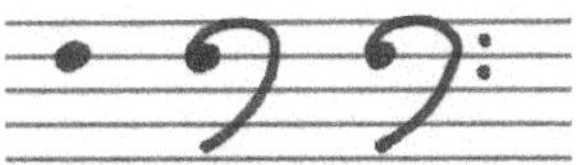

Draw 10 Bass clefs on the blank staff below.

4. Trace the bar lines (and double bar line) to create 4 measures on the Grand Staff below.

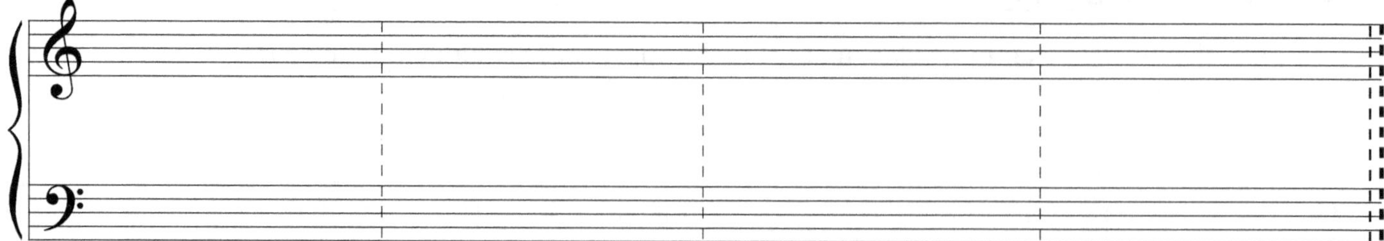

5. Add a Treble clef, Bass clef, bar lines and a double bar line to the Grand Staff below.

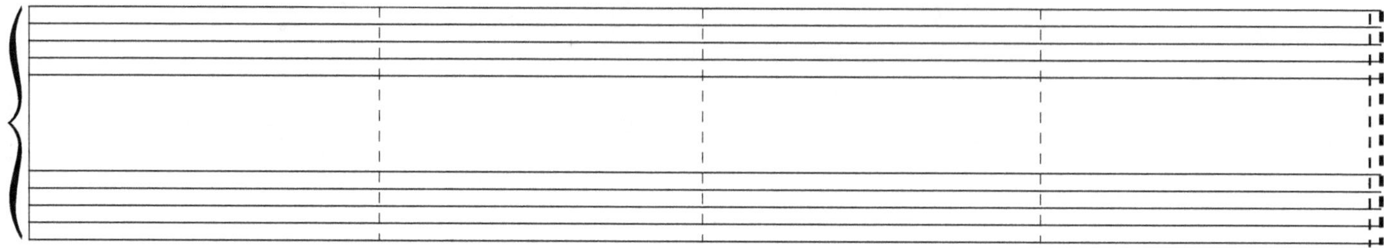

6. Add "up stems" to the following notes. Remember the notes should look like a lowercase "d."
The first one is done for you.

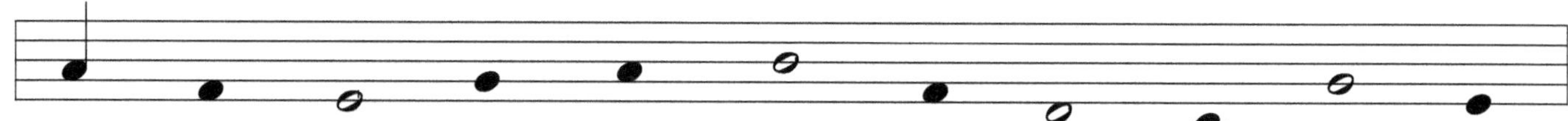

7. Add "down stems" to the following notes. Remember the notes should look like a lowercase "p."
The first one is done for you.

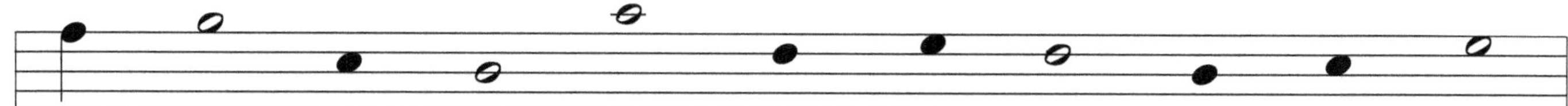

8. Add stems to the following notes. If the note head is below the middle line, the stem goes up, if the note head is above the middle line, the stem goes down. The notes on the middle line of the staff can have up or down stems.

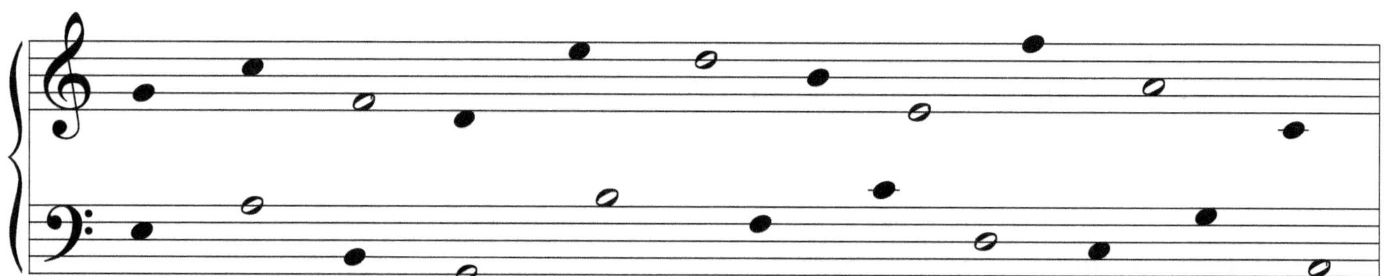

Lesson 4: Time Signatures & Beats

A Time Signature tells us how many beats are in each measure of music (top number), and what type of note receives one beat (bottom number). In this lesson, all time signatures have a 4 as the bottom number. The 4 on the bottom means a quarter note receives 1 beat.

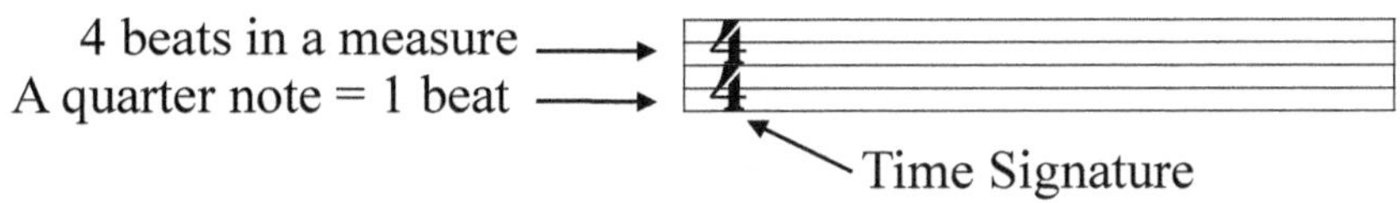

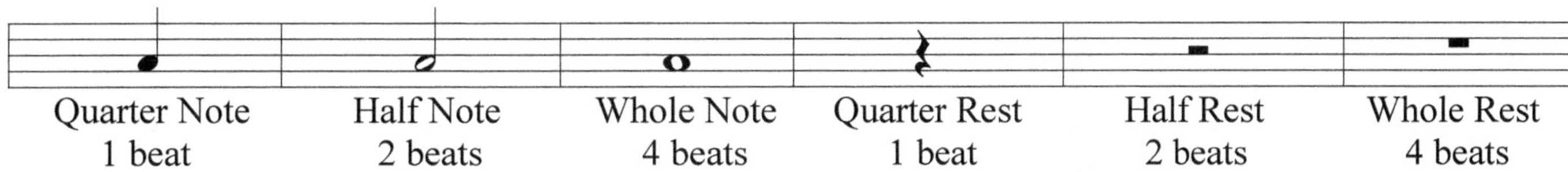

*Rests share the same name and value as notes, but are silent beats.

In the following examples, each measure contains the correct number of beats according to the time signature, and the beats are written underneath the notes/rests. Notice how the rests get a beat, just like the notes, even though they are silent.

In this example, you count to 4 in the first measure, and when the bar line comes down, you start over, and count to 4 again.

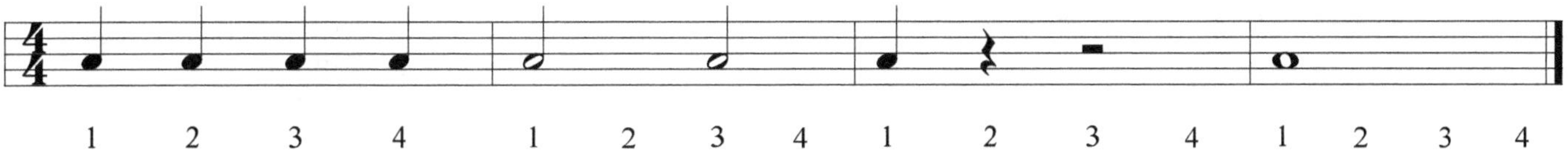

In this example, you count to 3 in the first measure, and when the bar line comes down, you start over, and count to 3 again.

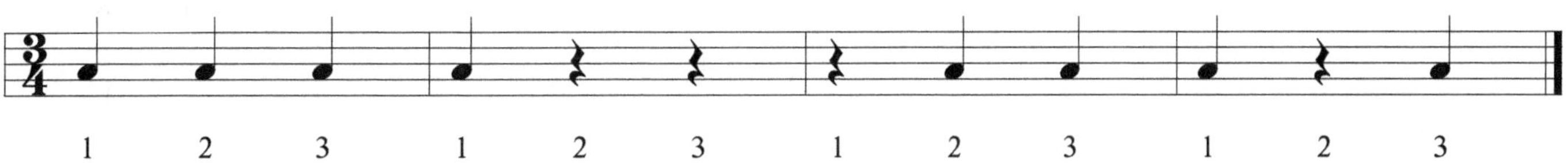

In this example, you count to 2 in the first measure, and when the bar line comes down, you start over, and count to 2 again.

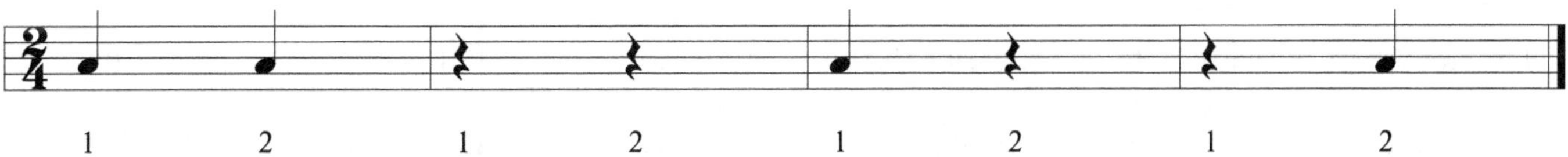

*Here's a trick to remember the difference between a half rest and a whole rest. The half rest looks like a top hat, ( ) so think "Half-Hat." The whole rest looks like you could walk along the staff and fall in a hole, ( ) so think "Whole-hole."

Review: Lesson 4

1. Check the correct counting for each of these examples.

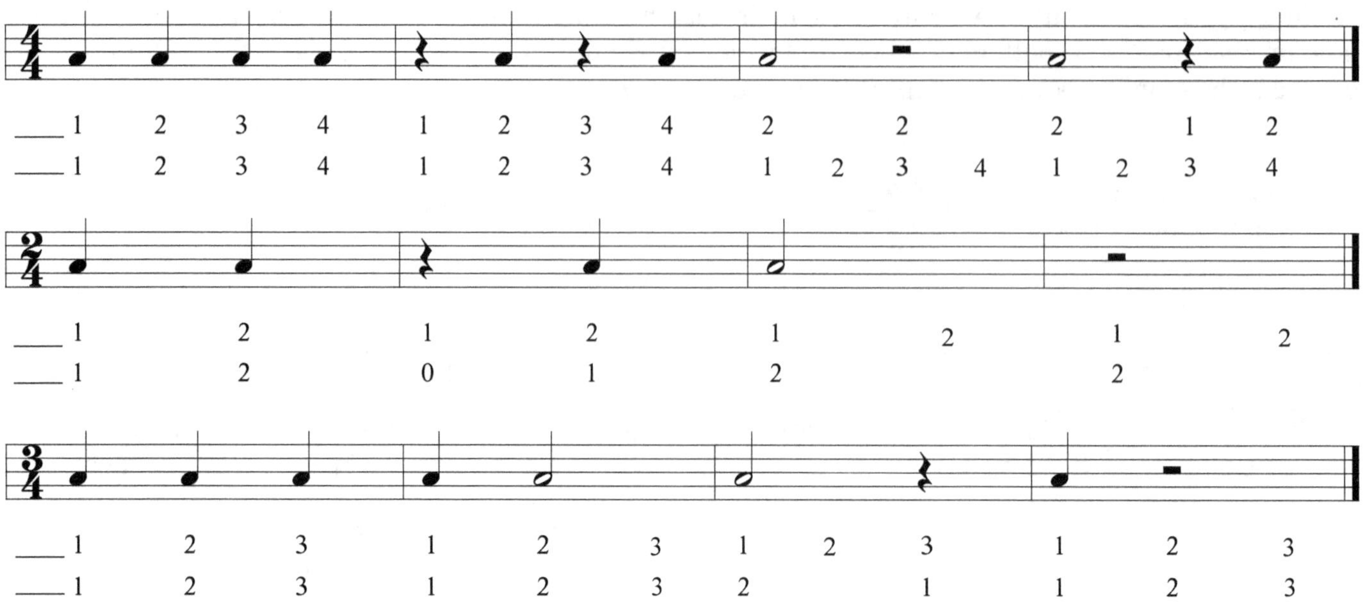

2. Check the correct number of beats each note or rest will receive in $\frac{4}{4}$ time.

3. Circle the correct name for each note or rest.

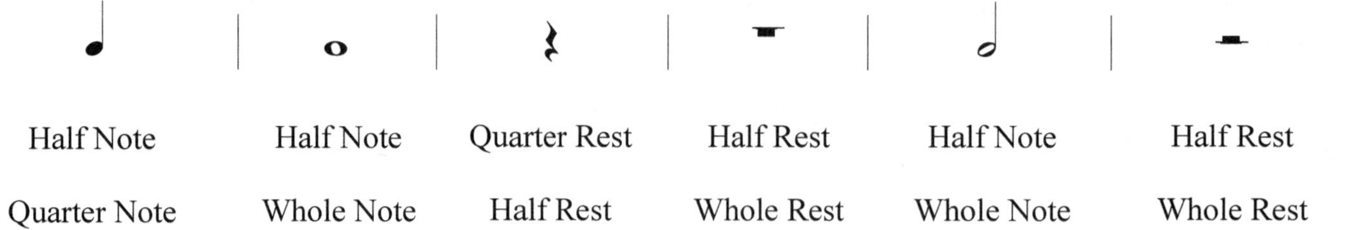

4. Add two missing bar lines and a double bar line to the following rhythms. Pay attention to the time signature changes. *It helps to write the beats under the notes.* The first measure is done for you.

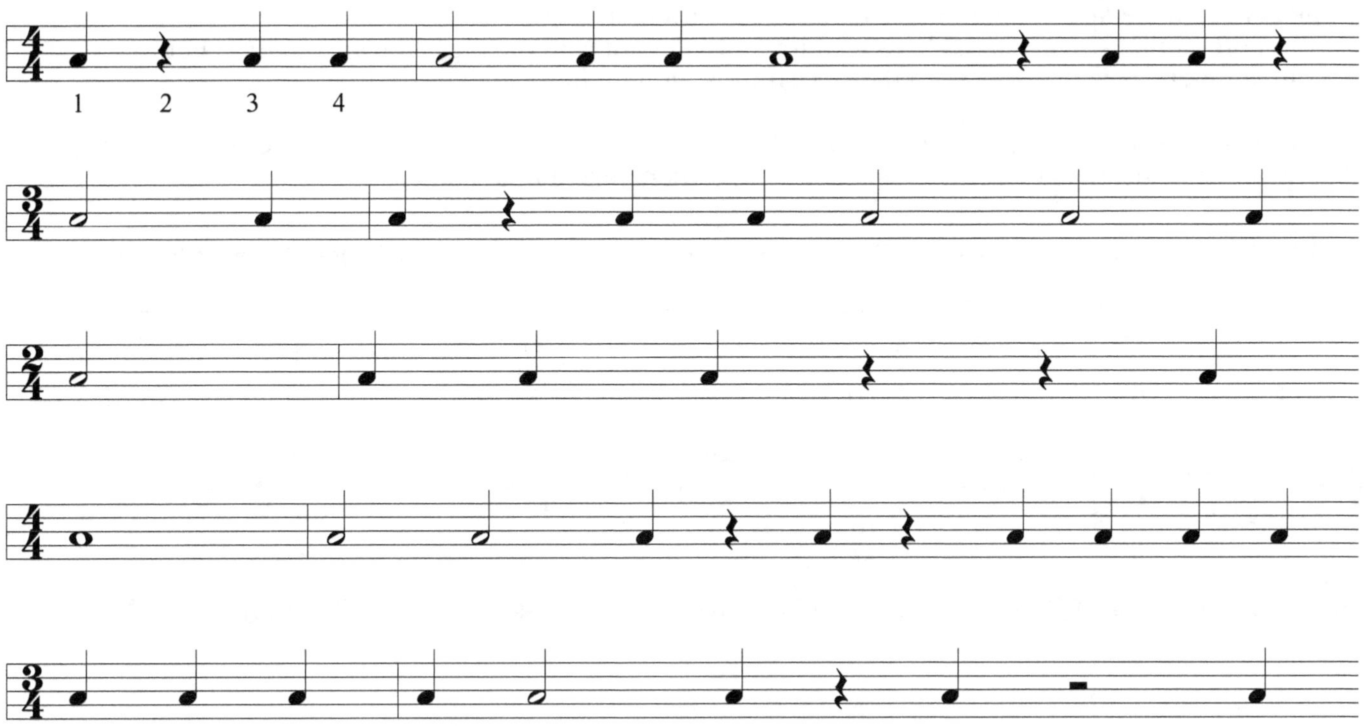

5. Add one missing note or rest to each measure to complete the necessary beats. Pay attention to the top number of each time signature.

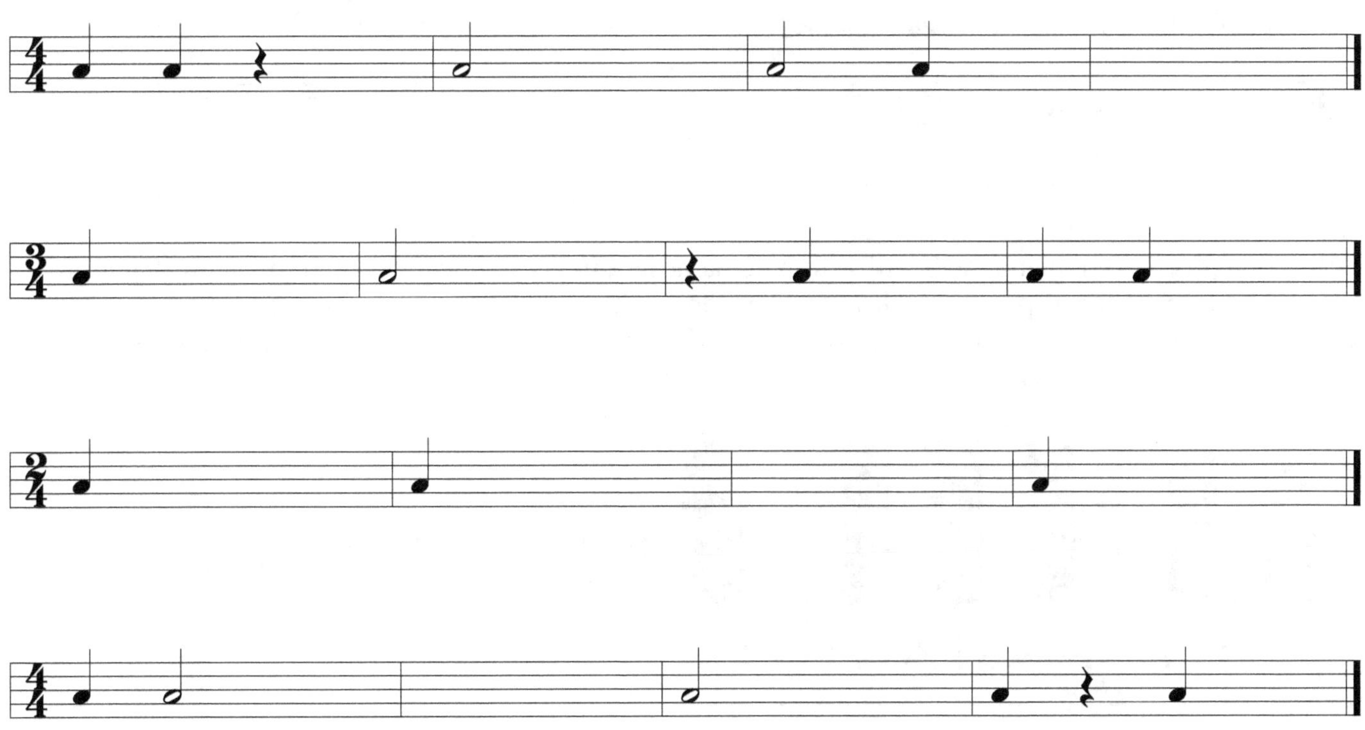

Lesson 5: Notes on the Grand Staff

Notes are written on the grand staff in order to enable musicians to read the music they are learning. Singers need to be able to read music in order to learn their parts.
It is important that singers are able to read not only the notes in the clef they are singing, but in the accompaniment as well. This is so they can follow along while they are singing.

The following staves contain notes in the Treble and Bass clefs. Notes can be on lines or in spaces. There are some useful sayings that can help with remembering note names.

Treble Clef Lined Notes: Every Good Boy Deserves Fudge **Treble Clef Spaced Notes:** FACE

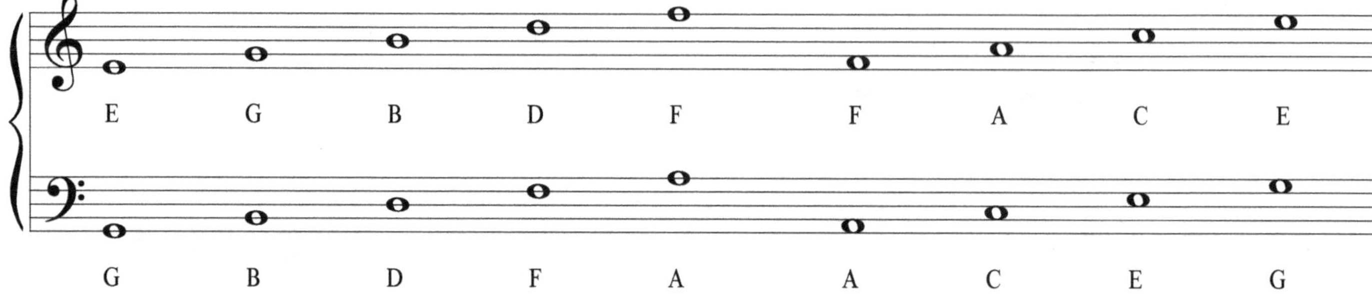

Bass Clef Lined Notes: Good Brownies Don't Fall Apart **Bass Clef Spaced Notes:** All Cows Eat Grass

Notes in order on the Grand Staff

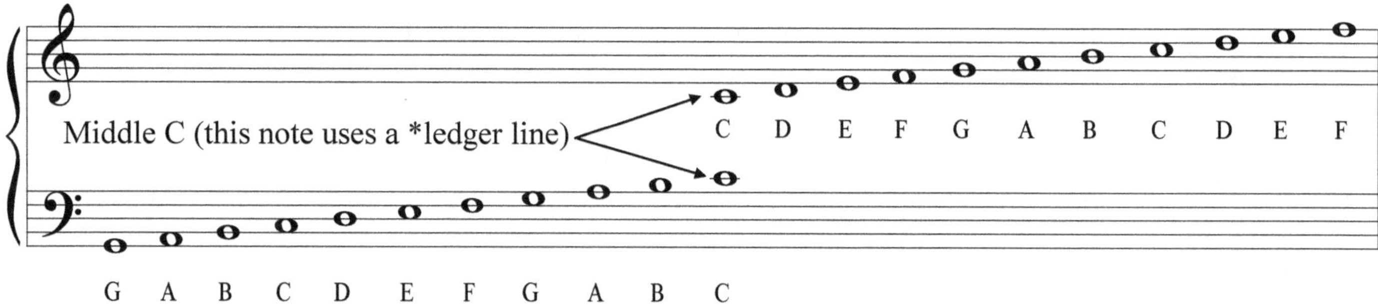

Below is a picture of a piano keyboard with note names on it. As singers, it is often difficult to picture musical concepts such as pitch, the distance between pitches, etc. Throughout these books, you will see piano keyboards like the one below to help clarify these concepts. As a singer, learning how to play the piano is an invaluable tool!

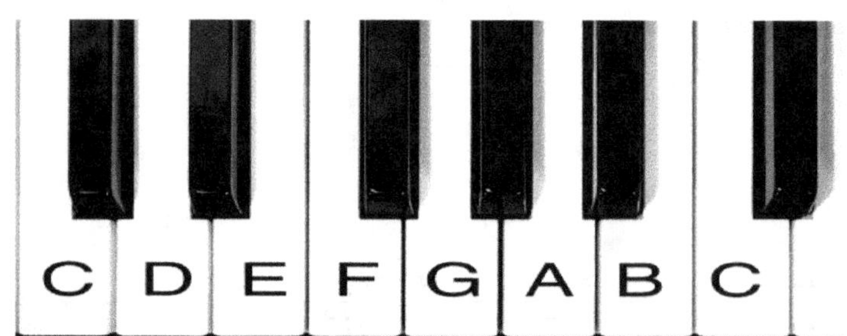

Notice how the pattern of notes: A-B-C-D-E-F-G repeats on the keyboard as it also does on the staves above.

*Short lines added above or below the staff so that notes can be written there. These will be defined further in Level 2.

Review: Lesson 5

1. Name the following spaced notes in the Treble clef. Look on the previous page for helpful sayings if you need help!

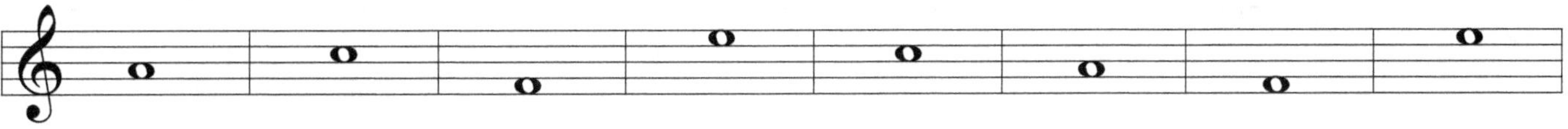

2. Name the following lined notes in the Treble clef.

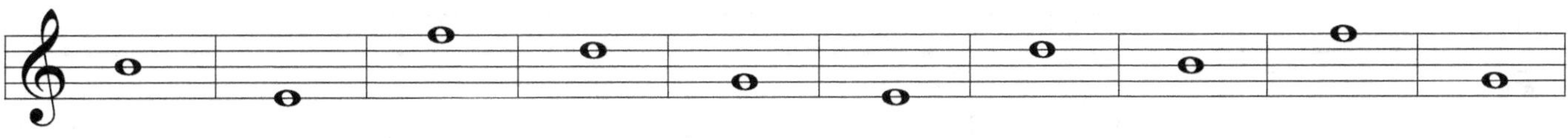

3. Name the following spaced notes in the Bass clef.

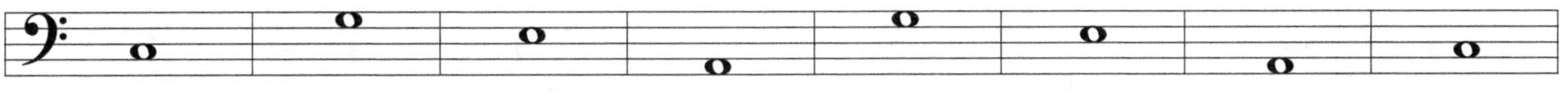

4. Name the following lined notes in the Bass clef.

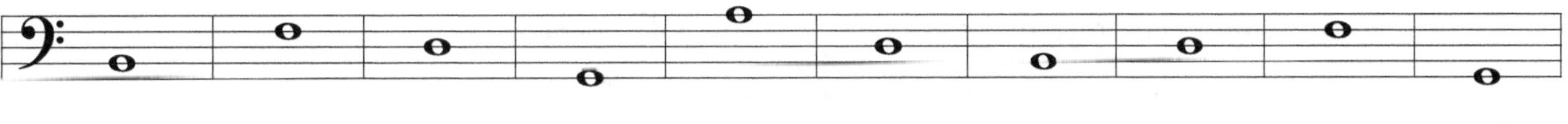

5. Name the following notes in the Treble clef.

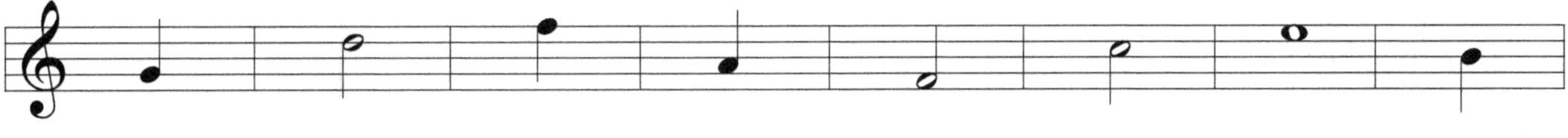

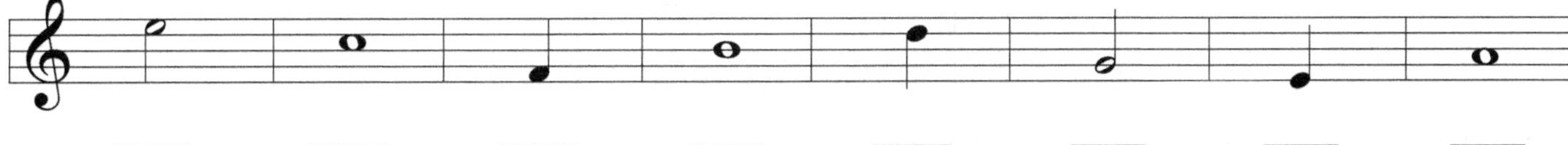

6. Name the following notes in the Bass clef.

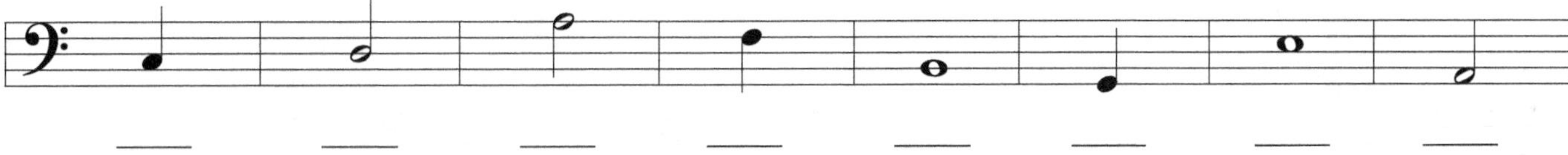

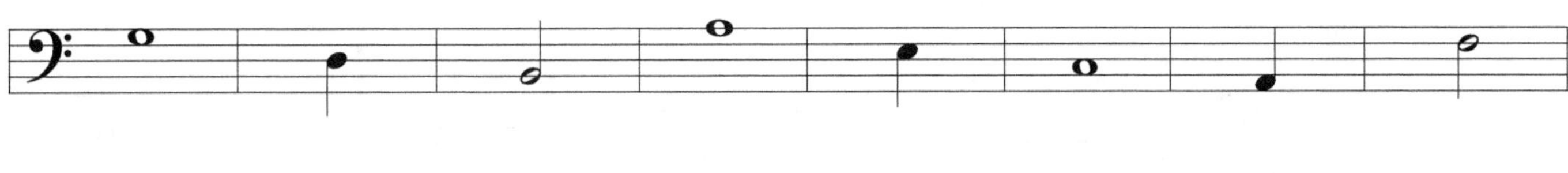

7. Draw the following <u>spaced</u> notes in the Treble clef. Use whole notes.

F A C E A F E C

8. Draw the following <u>lined</u> notes in the Treble clef. Use whole notes.

E G B D F B E D G F

9. Draw the following <u>spaced</u> notes in the Bass clef. Use whole notes.

A C E G C E A G

10. Draw the following <u>lined</u> notes in the Bass clef. Use whole notes.

G B D F A D G F A B

11. Write the letter name of each note.

____ ____ ____ ____ ____ ____ ____ ____

____ ____ ____ ____ ____ ____ ____ ____

Lesson 6: Key Signatures

In music, a Key Signature is a series of sharp (♯) or flat (♭) symbols placed on the staff immediately after the Treble and Bass clefs. The Key Signature also creates the tonal center for a piece.

The key signature shows which notes are to be played a half step higher (sharp) or a half step lower (flat) for the duration of the piece.

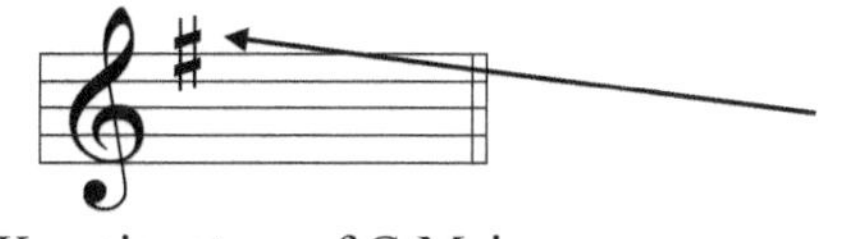
Key signature of G Major

This sharp sign means that all F's are to be sung as an F♯ (a half step higher).

A half step is the distance from one pitch the the very next pitch (up or down), while a whole step is comprised of 2 half steps (up or down). This is easy to see on a piano keyboard like the one below.

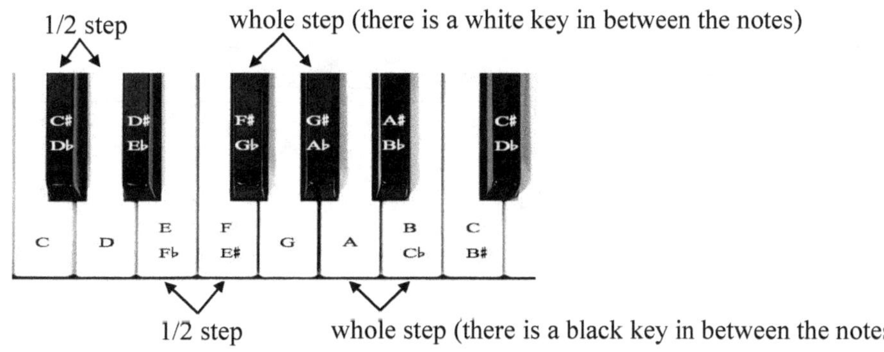

The key signature of G Major has an F♯ because in order for it to sound Major (or happy), the notes must follow a specific pattern of half steps and whole steps.

The pattern of half steps and whole steps that make up a Major scale (8 notes) is as follows:

Whole - Whole - Half - Whole - Whole - Whole - Half (W - W - H - W - W - W - H)

Take a look at a G Major scale on the staff below. The F♯ must be added in order for the formula (pattern of half steps and whole steps) to be correct.

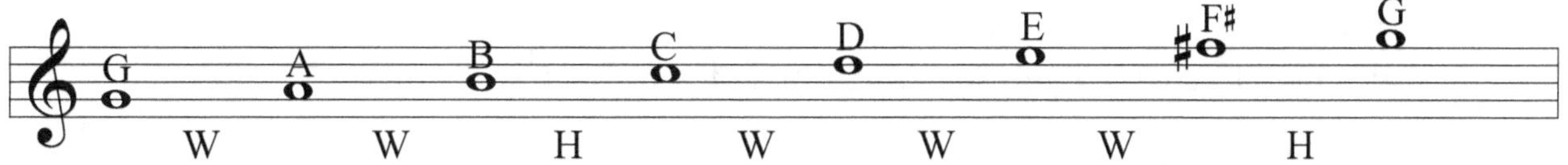

Here is what a G Major scale looks like on a piano keyboard.

- G to A is a whole step (there is a black note in between, G to A consists of 2 half steps).
- A to B is a whole step
- B to C is a half step (no note in between, they are as close as they can be)
- C to D is a whole step
- D to E is a whole step
- E to F♯ is a whole step (we had to add the sharp because E to F would only be a half step, which wouldn't be correct in our Major scale formula).
- F♯ to G is a half step

In this Level, we are going to study 4 different key signatures: C Major, G Major, D Major & F Major.

Look at the Major scales below for these key signatures so you can see how the Major scale pattern, W-W-H-W-W-W-H adds the necessary accidentals (sharps/flats).

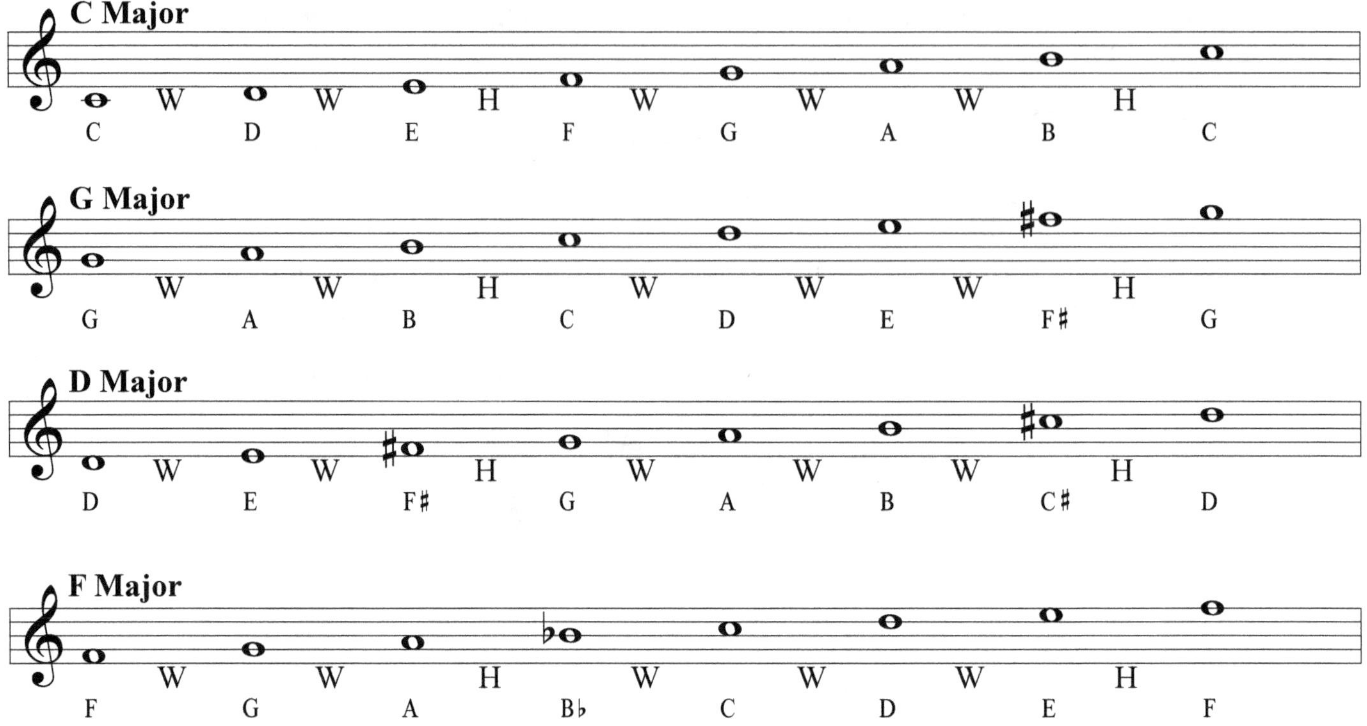

Here are the key signatures for the scales.

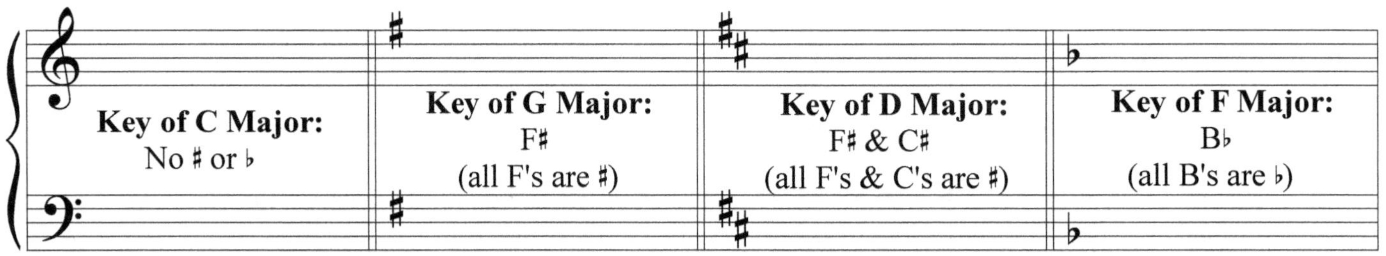

Here is what the scales look like with a key signature The notes with a ♯/♭ are circled.

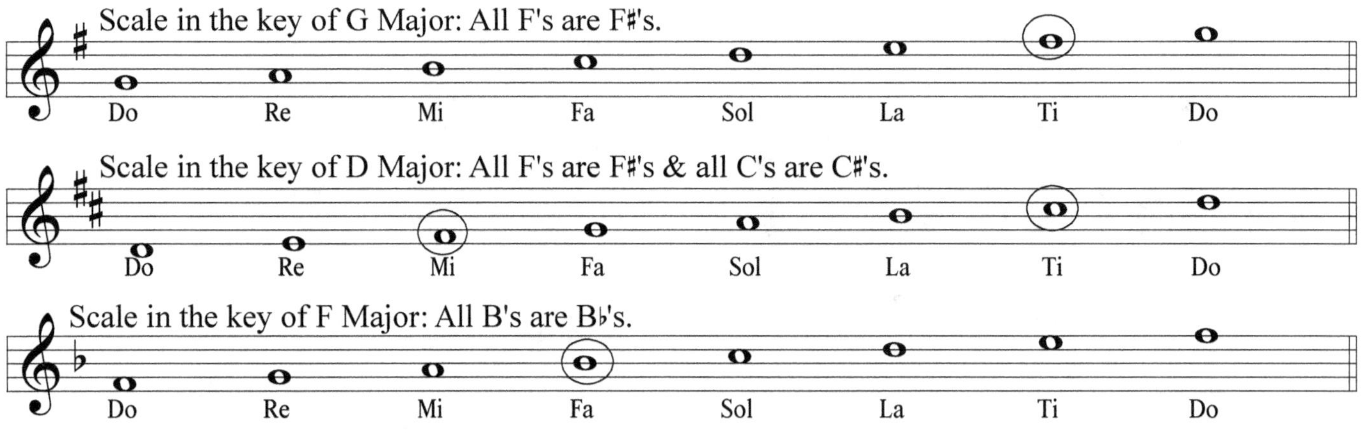

If you don't remember the formula for the Major scale, here are some additional tools for remembering how to identify a key signature.

For sharp keys (key signatures with sharps), there are two easy ways to identify a key signature.

1. Look at the last sharp (farthest one to the right), then name the next note in the musical alphabet. That's the key! In D Major, for example, the farthest sharp to the right is C♯. The next letter in the musical alphabet is D, so the key is D Major.

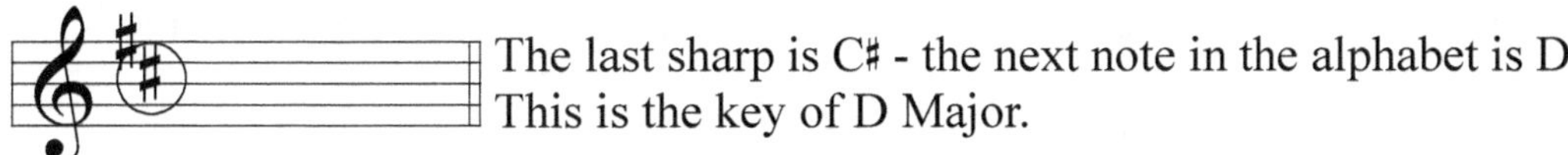

The last sharp is C♯ - the next note in the alphabet is D
This is the key of D Major.

2. Look at the last sharp (farthest to the right), and it is the "Ti" in the Major scale. If the last sharp (farthest to the right) is "Ti" then "Do" is the next note. In the key of G Major, F♯ is the last sharp in the key signature, so it is "Ti." If F♯ is "Ti" then G is "Do." The key is G Major.

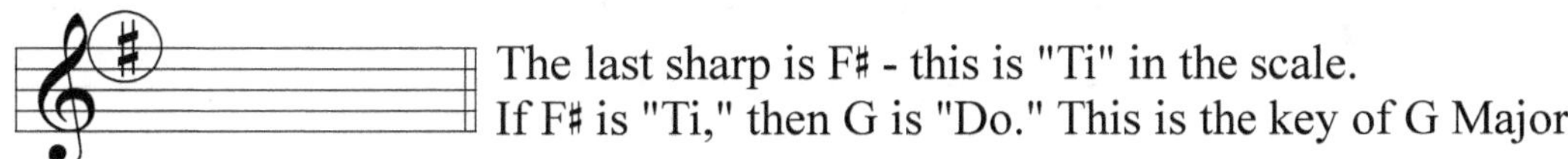

The last sharp is F♯ - this is "Ti" in the scale.
If F♯ is "Ti," then G is "Do." This is the key of G Major.

There are two remaining keys in this lesson; C Major and F Major.

C Major has no sharps and flats, so there are none in its key signature.

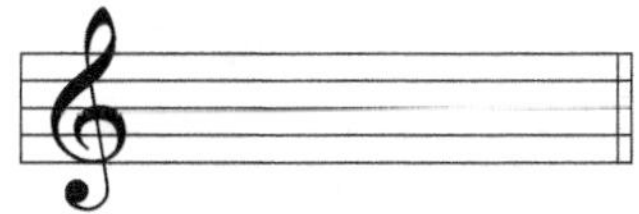

F Major has one flat. Other than memorizing this, there is one tool that can help you figure out the key when there are flats in the key signature.

1. Look at the last flat, it is "Fa" of the Major scale. From there, you can count up to "Do" to figure out the key.

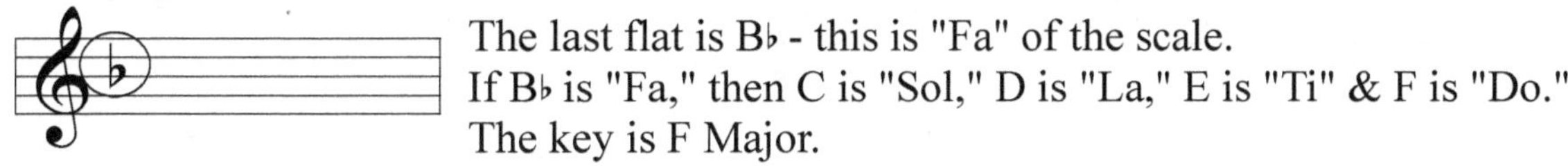

The last flat is B♭ - this is "Fa" of the scale.
If B♭ is "Fa," then C is "Sol," D is "La," E is "Ti" & F is "Do."
The key is F Major.

*When sharps or flats appear in a key signature, <u>all</u> sharped or flatted notes are affected; they do not have to be on the same line or space that the sharp and flat are on in the key signature.

For instance, in the key of G Major, <u>all</u> F's are F♯'s, not just the F on the top line of the Treble staff and the 4th line of the Bass staff.

Review: Lesson 6

1. Circle the correct pattern of Whole steps and Half steps that create a Major scale.

   a. W H W W W H W

   b. W W H W W W H

2. Add the necessary ♯ or ♭ to the scales below to create Major scales. Make sure you draw the ♯/♭ before the note that is affected. The center part of the sharp and flat must be on the same line/space of the note it is affecting.

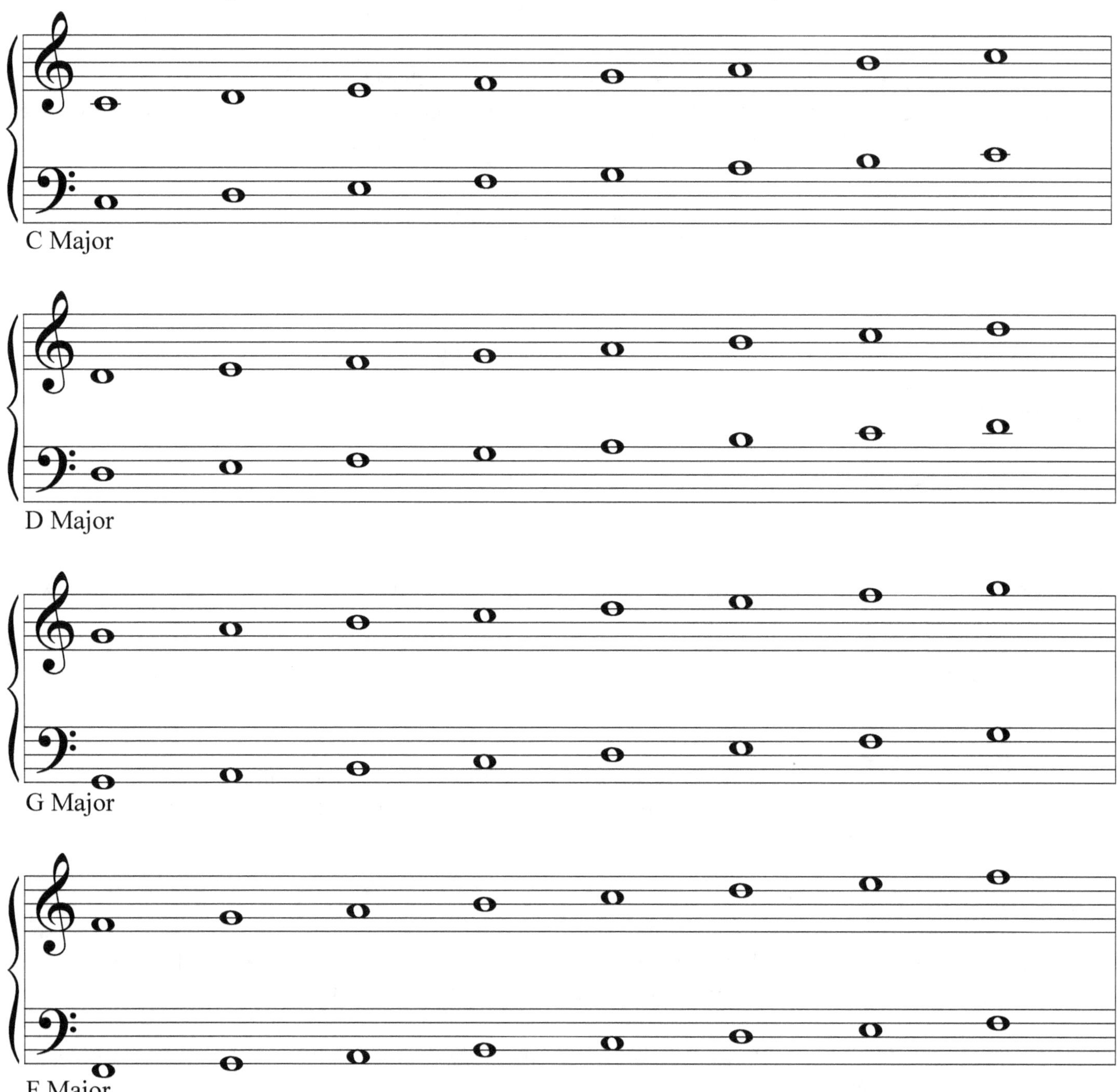

3. Name the Major key for each of these key signatures. The first one is done for you.

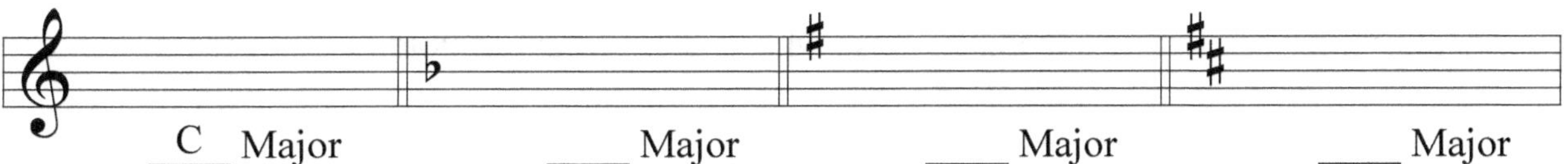

C Major ____ Major ____ Major ____ Major

4. Draw the key signature in both the Treble and Bass staves for each of the requested keys. Make sure you add the ♯/♭ to the correct line/space and keep the center part of the ♯/♭ on the correct line/space. Look at question 3 for hints.

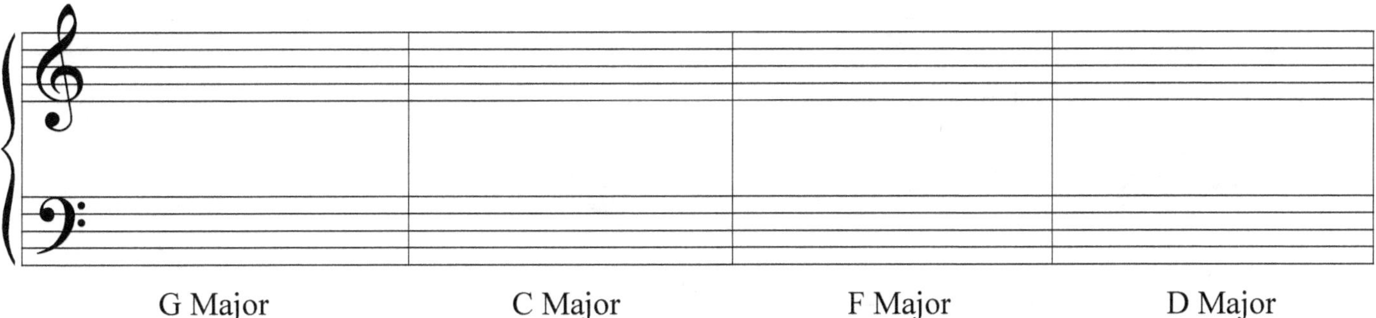

G Major C Major F Major D Major

5. Circle the notes affected the by key signature. Pay attention to clef changes.

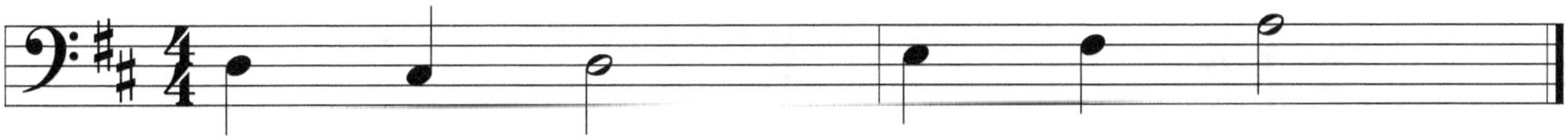

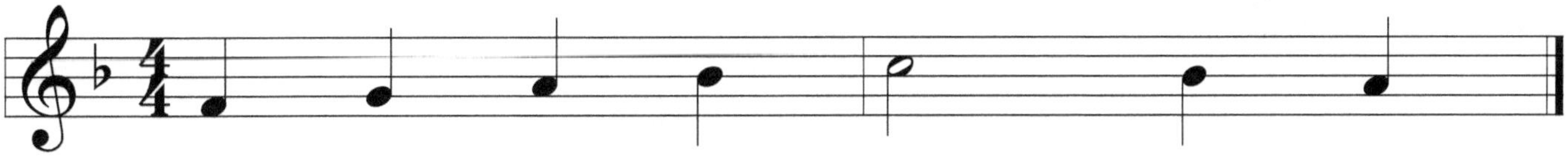

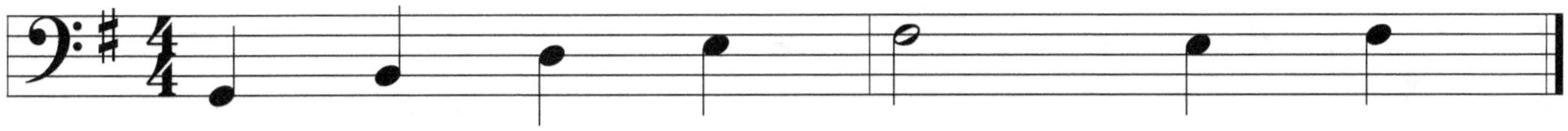

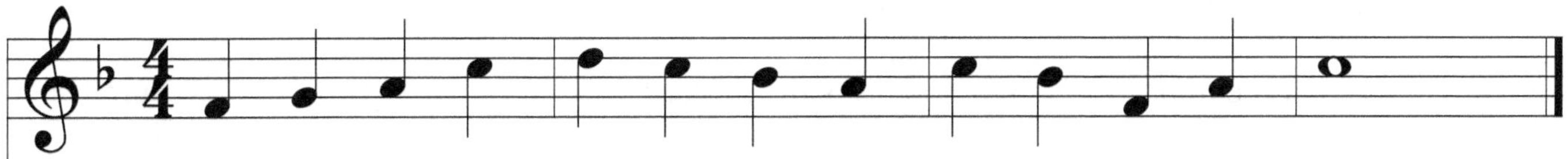

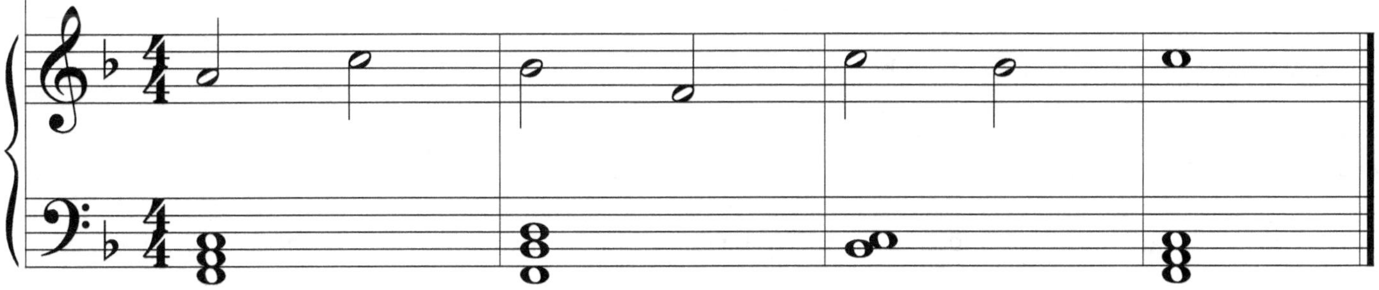

Review: Lessons 1-6

1. Draw a treble clef, followed by ten lined notes. Use whole, half or quarter notes.

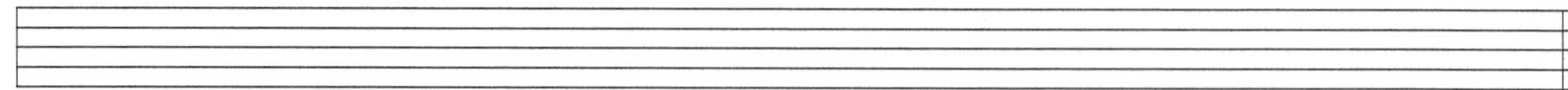

2. Draw a bass clef, followed by ten spaced notes. Use whole, half or quarter notes.

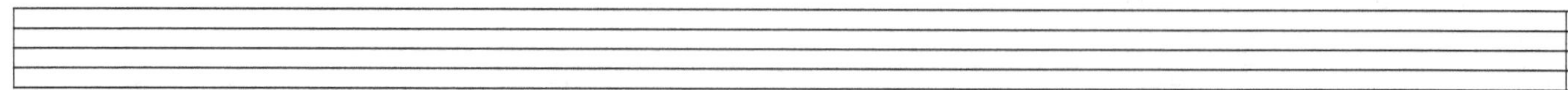

3. Match the number of each musical symbol with its name.

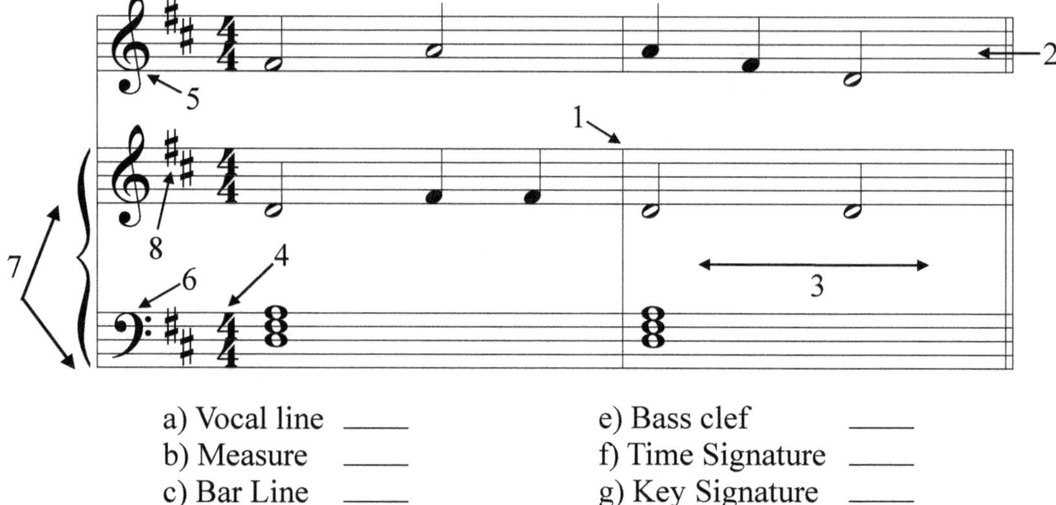

a) Vocal line ____
b) Measure ____
c) Bar Line ____
d) Treble clef ____
e) Bass clef ____
f) Time Signature ____
g) Key Signature ____
h) Piano Accompaniment ____

4. Add stems to the following notes.

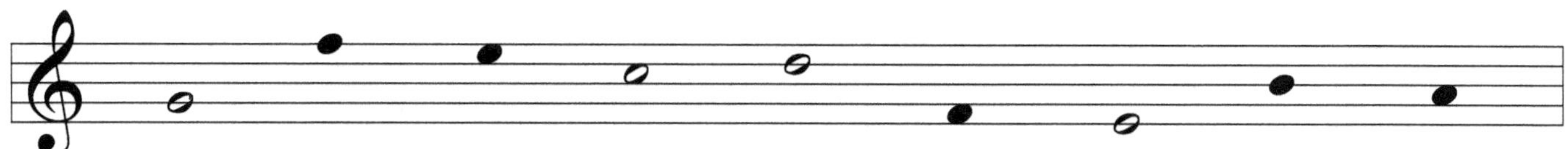

5. Fill in the blanks regarding the Time Signatures below.

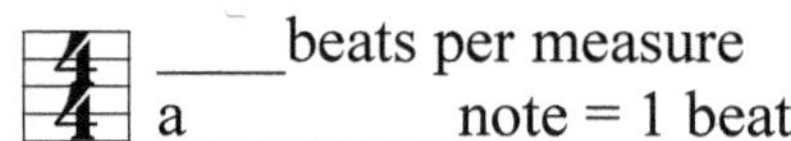
____beats per measure
a ________note = 1 beat

____beats per measure
a ________note = 1 beat

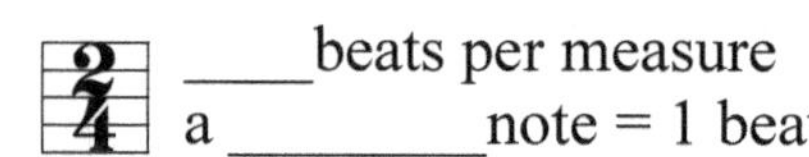
____beats per measure
a ________note = 1 beat

6. Name the note/rest and how many beats it has.

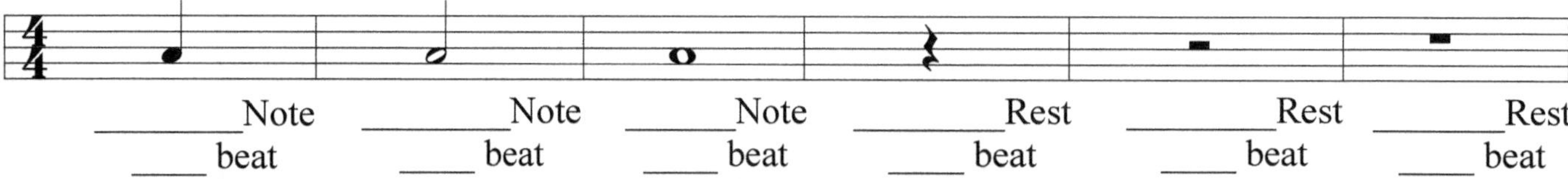

________Note ____ beat
________Note ____ beat
______Note ____ beat
________Rest ____ beat
________Rest ____ beat
________Rest ____ beat

7. Check the correct counting for the example below.

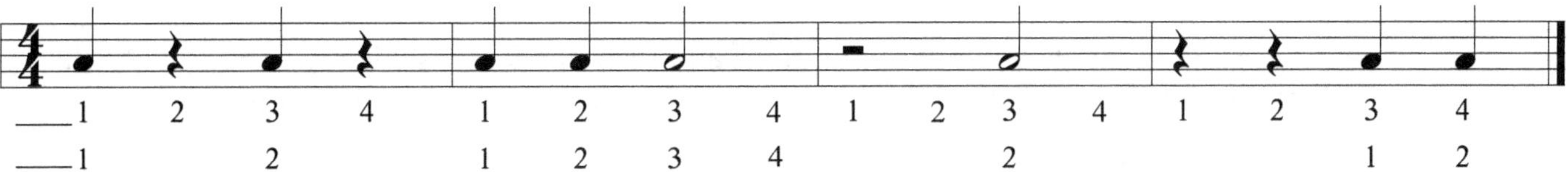

8. Add 3 missing bar lines and a double bar line to the following rhythm.

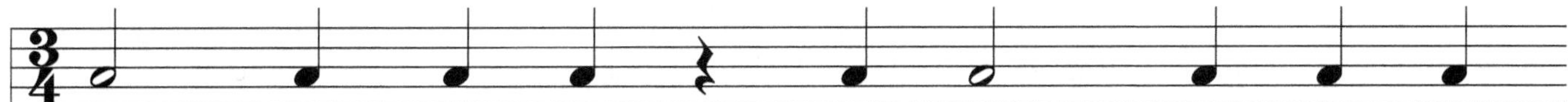

9. Add one missing note or rest to each measure to complete the necessary beats.

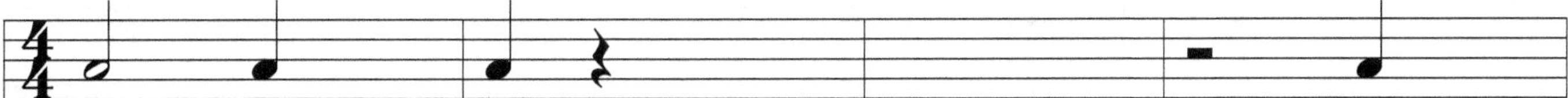

10. Write the letter name of each note.

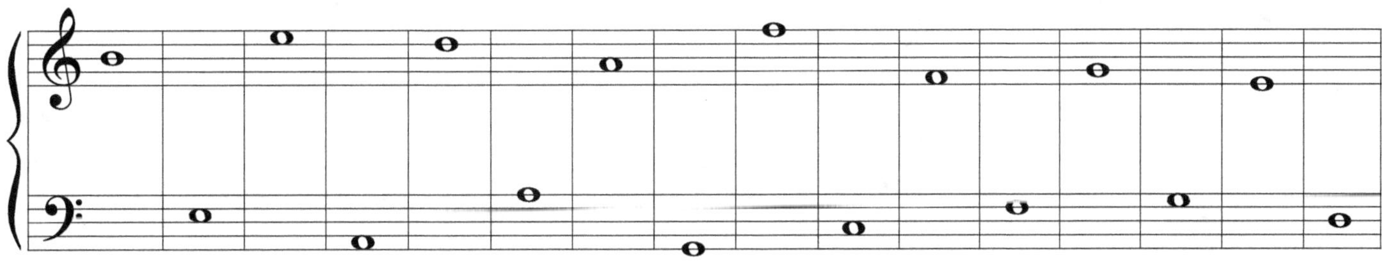

___ ___ ___ ___ ___ ___ ___ ___ ___ ___ ___ ___ ___ ___ ___ ___

11. Add the necessary ♯ or ♭ to the scales below to create Major scales.

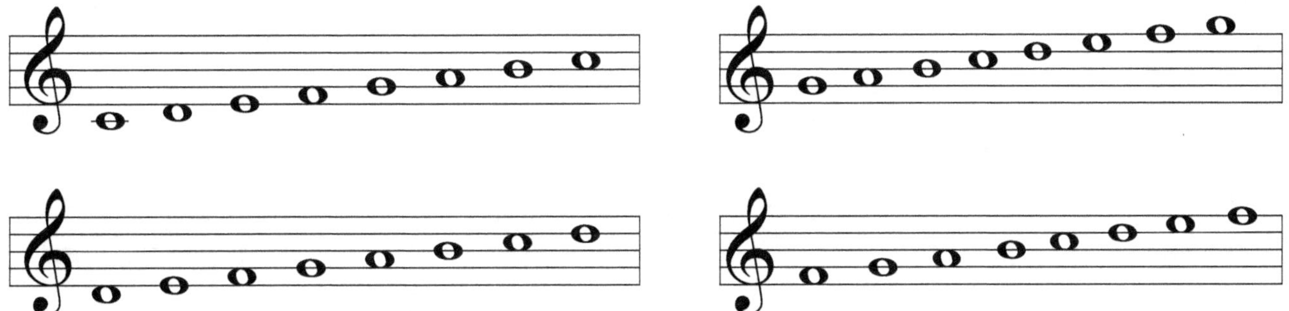

12. Name the Major key for each of these key signatures.

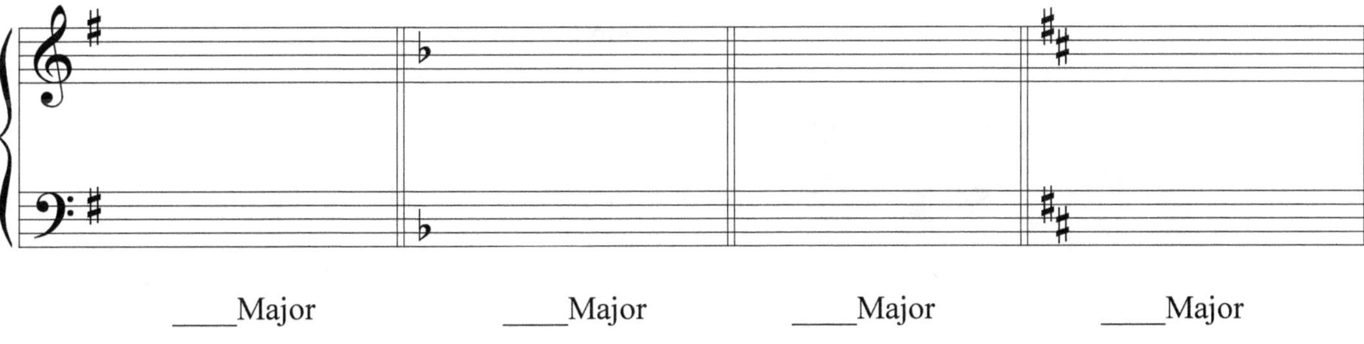

Lesson 7: Triads

A Triad, or 3-note chord, is formed when the first, third and fifth notes of a scale are sung or played, either consecutively or at the same time. The root, or the lowest note of a triad, determines its letter name.

Example: C Major. C is the 1st/root, E is the 3rd/middle note, G is the 5th/top note

This is a "root position" chord

The following examples show the Major Scales and Major Triads formed on the first note of the scale (Do). The 1st, 3rd, & 5th notes (Do-Mi-Sol) are circled.

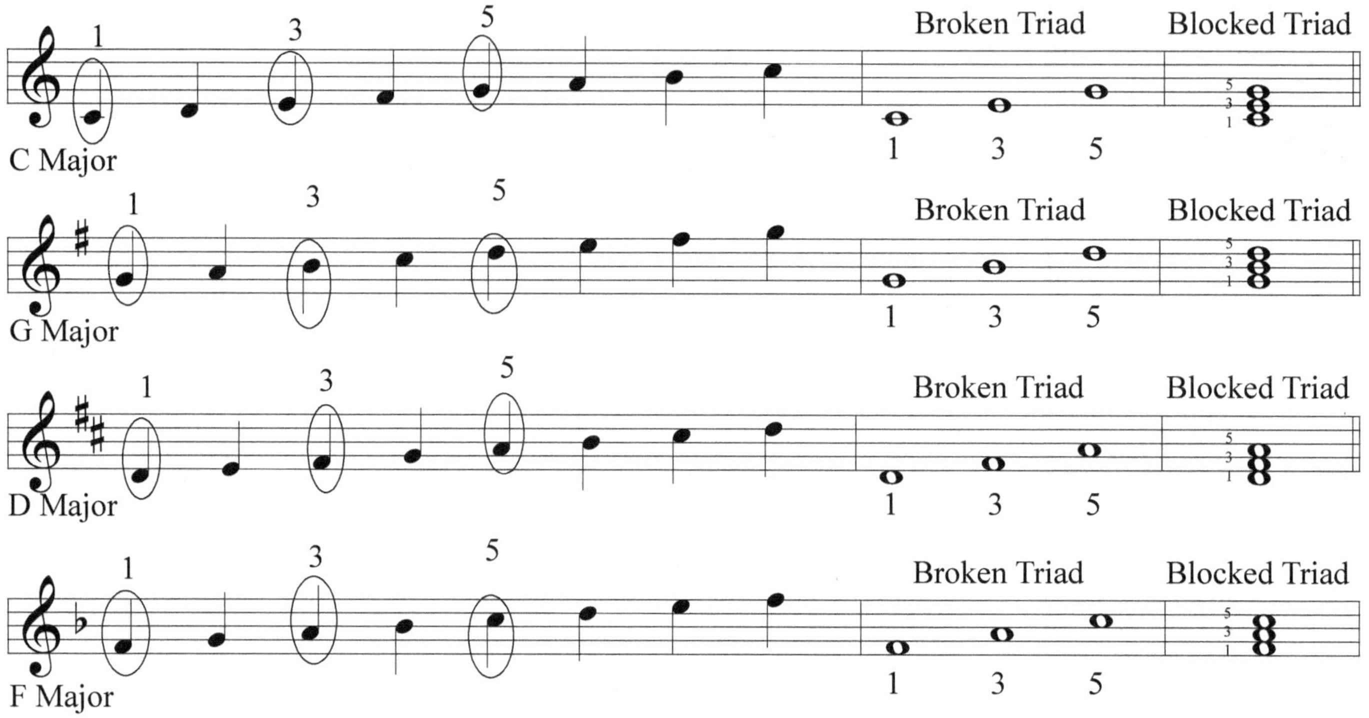

Here are the root position triads in both clefs.

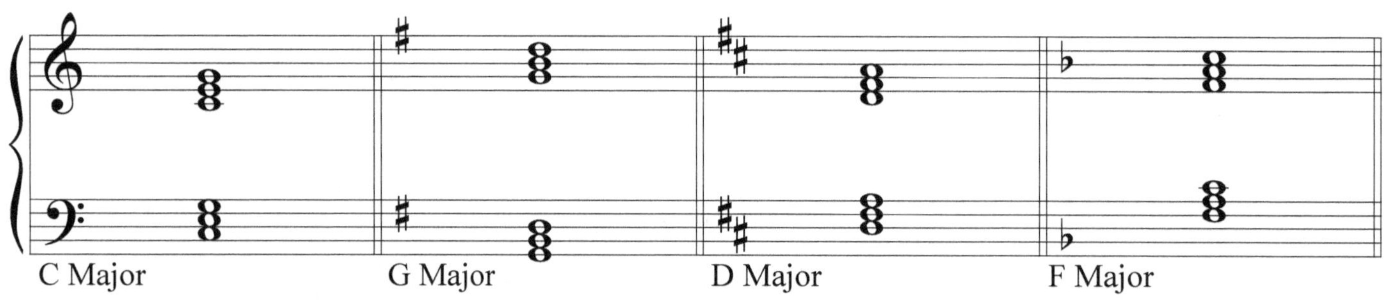

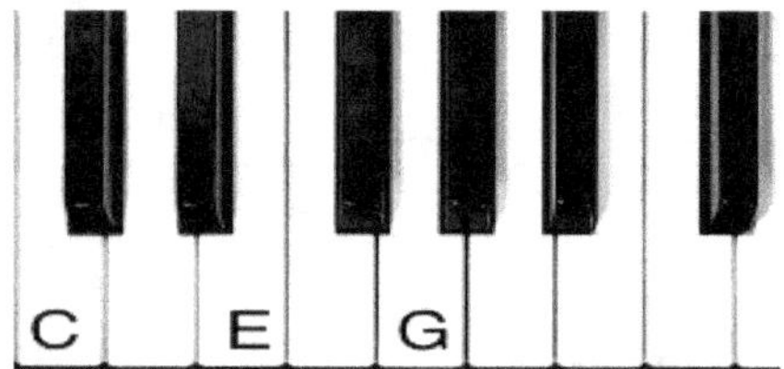

This is what a C Major Triad looks like on a piano keyboard.

Review: Lesson 7

1. Name the following triads. Remember, look at the bottom note (root) for the "name" of the triad.

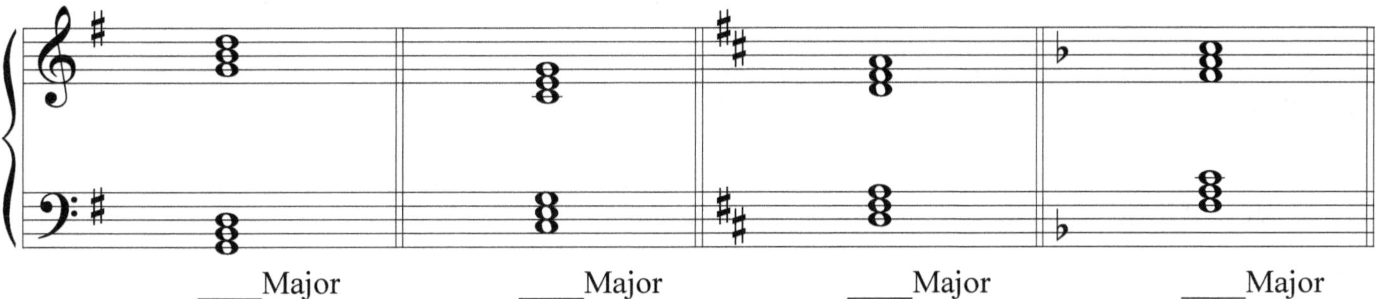

____Major ____Major ____Major ____Major

2. For the following examples, draw the correct key signature, then add the root position triads to both the Treble and Bass clefs. Look at question 1 for hints.

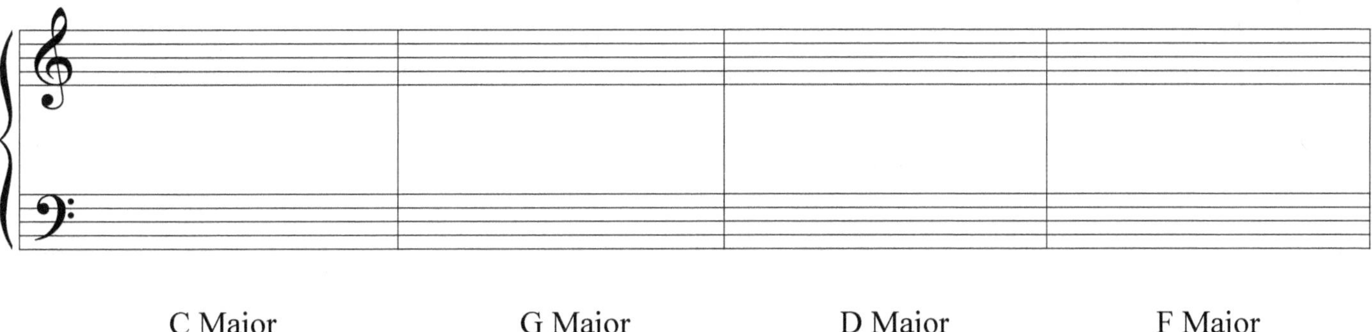

C Major G Major D Major F Major

3. Circle the three notes in the scale below that make up a root position triad.

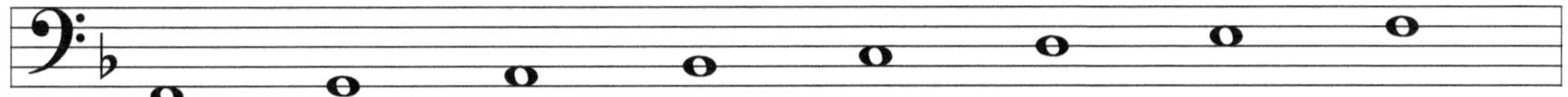

4. Each of these triads should have 3 notes (Do-Mi-Sol/root-middle-top).
Fill in the missing note to create a root position triad for the given key.

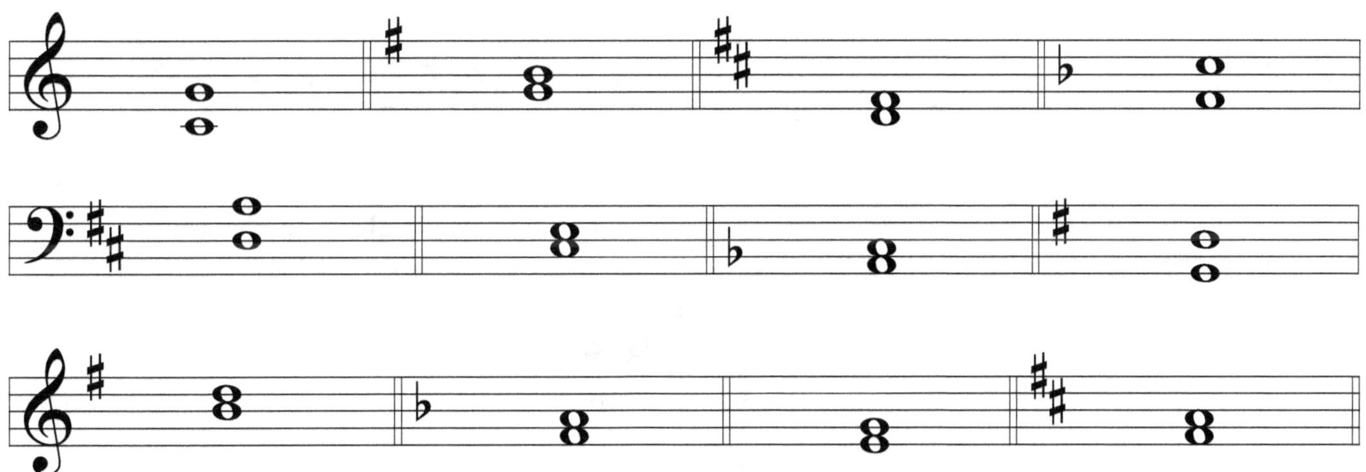

Lesson 8: Intervals (2nds & 3rds)

An Interval, in music, is the distance between any two notes. In this level, the intervals of a 2nd and 3rd will be covered. When counting intervals, be sure to include the bottom and top notes.

For singing, Do-Re is a 2nd, Do-Mi is a 3rd. Intervals are sung melodically (one note at a time), or harmonically (two notes at the same time - two singers singing at the same time).

Look at the examples below. Notice how the interval of a second has a line and a space note. The interval of a 3rd either has 2 line notes or 2 space notes.

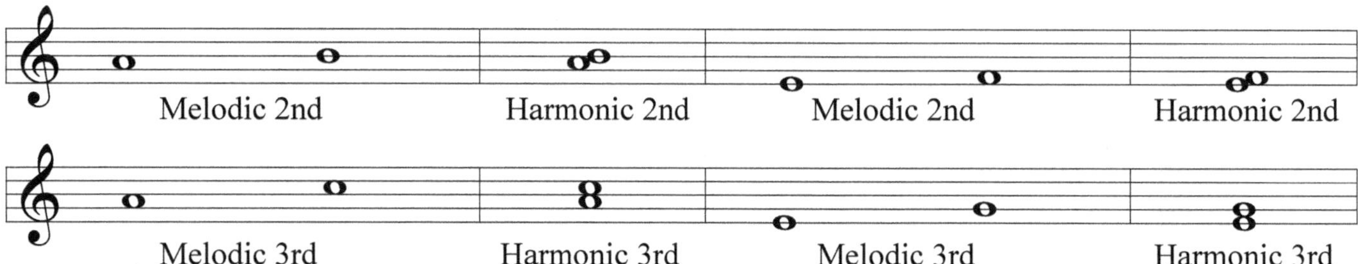

In singing, 2nds and 3rds use the following solfege.

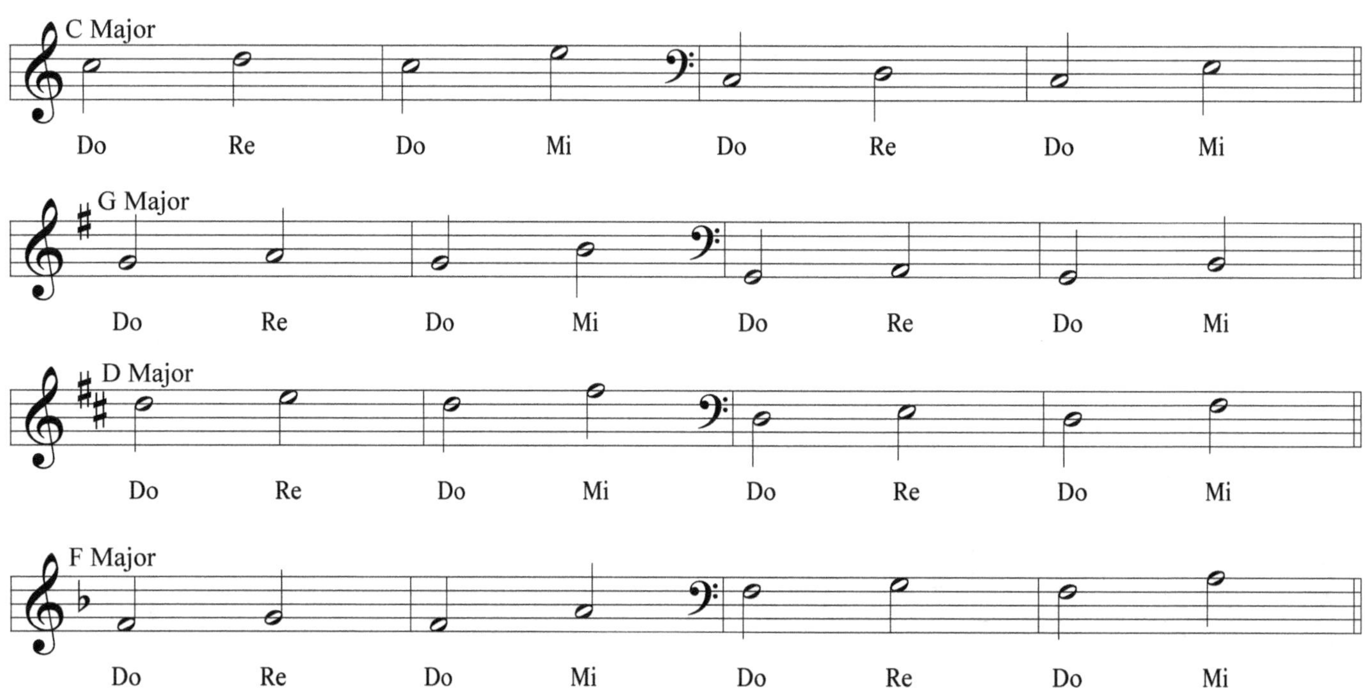

On the piano keyboard below, you can see the distance between the intervals. If you have a piano, keyboard, or piano app, play and sing these notes so you can hear the difference between the intervals.

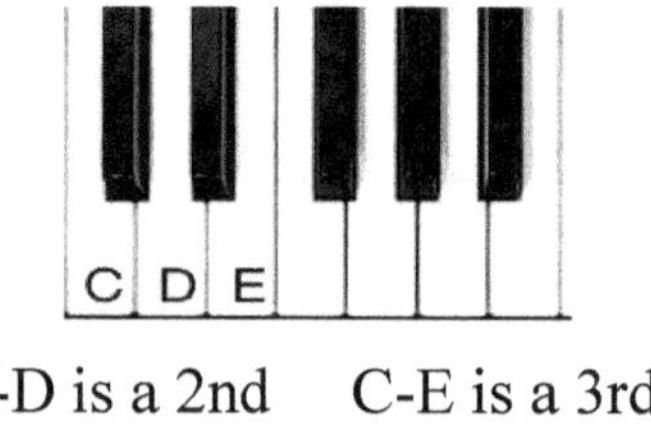

C-D is a 2nd   C-E is a 3rd

Review: Lesson 8

1. Circle all of the harmonic 2nds.

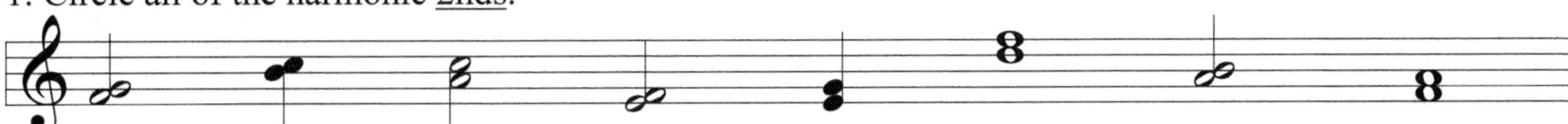

2. Circle all of the harmonic 3rds.

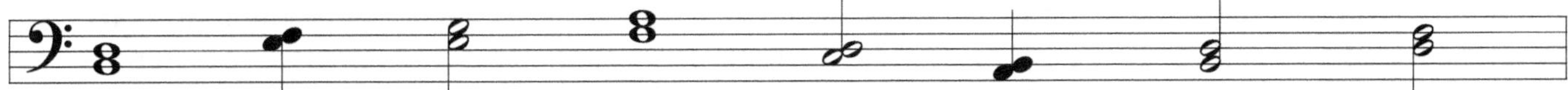

3. Label each melodic interval as a 2nd or 3rd.

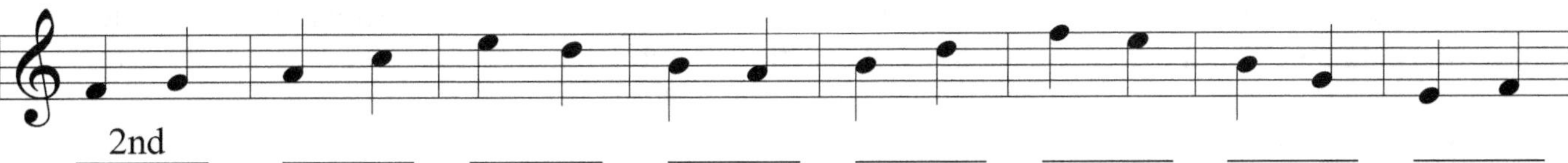

4. Name each interval: 2nd or 3rd.

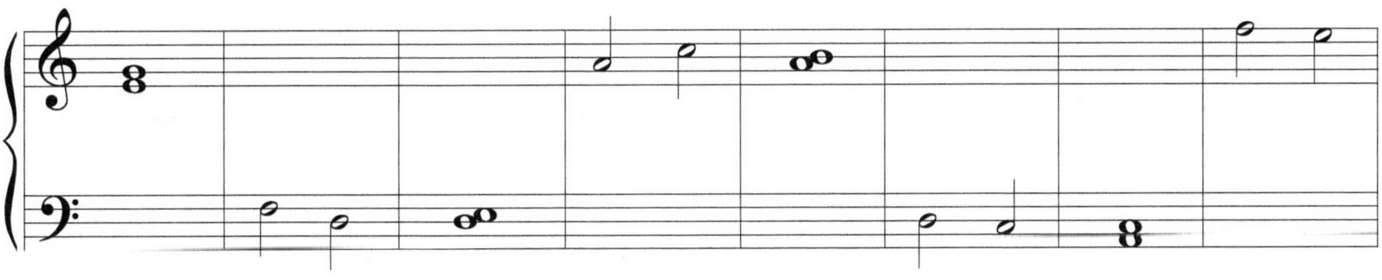

5. Add one note per measure to complete the requested melodic intervals.
Add the note after and above the given note. Make sure you add stems in the correct direction.
Use half notes. The first one is done for you.

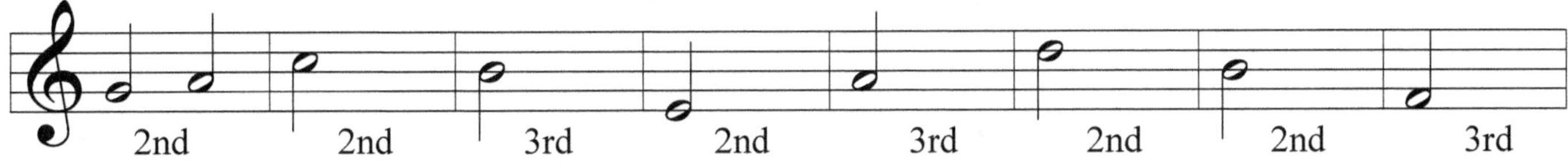

6. Add one note per measure to complete the requested melodic intervals.
Add the note after and below the given note. Make sure you add stems in the correct direction.
Use quarter notes. The first one is done for you.

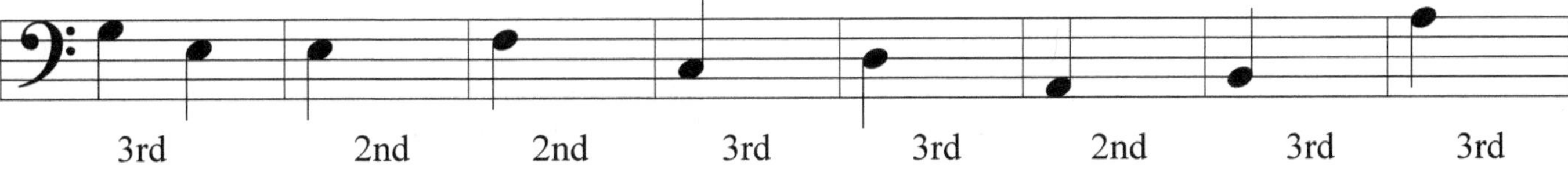

7. Add one note per measure to complete the requested harmonic intervals.
Add the note above the given note. 2nds go above and next to the given note.
Use whole notes. The first one is done for you.

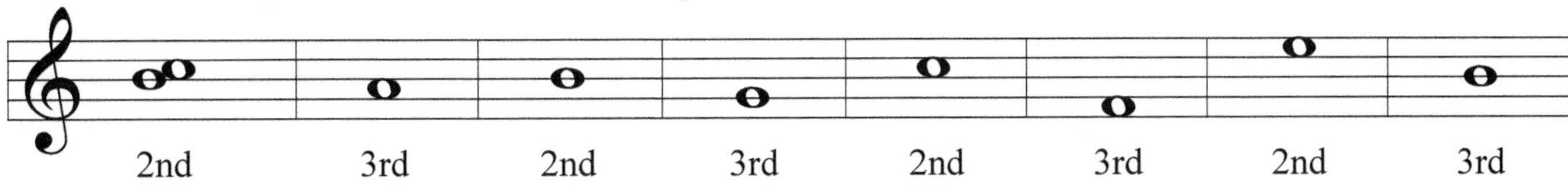

Lesson 9: Vocal Diction & IPA

Every time we sing a song, we are telling a story. As singers, we have to be exceptionally clear with how we pronounce the words of our songs, or our audience will not understand us, and our story will not be told.

If you reference a dictionary in any Latin based language (English, Italian, French, German, Spanish, Latin, etc.) you will see some symbols next to the words. These symbols make up the International Phonetic Alphabet, or IPA. The IPA represents the sounds of a language. In fact, the IPA represents nearly any vowel or consonant made by human beings!

In this lesson, we'll focus on a few of the vowel sounds in the IPA. You will learn what the letter looks like in our language, what the IPA symbol for that letter is, and what it sounds like.

Before we look at the symbols, make a couple of sounds so you can see all of the different positions your tongue moves to in order to make each sound.

Say "ah" as in the word "father," and "ee" as in the word "meet." You'll notice that when you say "ah," your tongue is at the bottom of your mouth, and when you say "ee" the center of your tongue moves to the roof of your mouth, while the tip remains down and behind the bottom teeth. When singing, we must be aware of any tension in our tongue, and ensure that it is in the proper position for creating accurate vowel sounds.

Here is a chart of the vowels we will learn in this lesson, along with their english equivalent.

IPA SYMBOL	SOUND IN ENGLISH WORD	IPA SPELLING OF WORD	TONGUE/LIPS PLACEMENT
i	ski	[ski]	Center of tongue is high Lips relaxed
ɛ	led	[lɛd]	Low tongue Lips relaxed
ɑ	father	[ˈfɑðər]	Low tongue Lips relaxed
o	obey	[oʊˈbeɪ]	Low tongue, tip behind bottom teeth Rounded lips
u	goose	[gus]	Low tongue, tip behind bottom teeth Rounded lips

courtesy of Sarah Sandvig

Practice saying the sounds above, and the english words in the second column.

Check that your tongue and lips are in the position described in the last column.

Additional IPA symbols, like the ones you see in the 3rd column will be introduced in later levels of these books.

Review: Lesson 9

1. Check the English word that contains the same sound as the given IPA symbol.

i ___Meet
___Mile

ɛ ___Peach
___Dress

ɑ ___Not
___Ate

o ___Thou
___Boat

u ___Ouch
___Loose

2. Circle the correct answer for the proper tongue and lip position for each IPA symbol. Say each sound, it will help!

i - Tongue is - high- and lips are - relaxed -
- low - - rounded -

ɛ - Tongue is - high- and lips are - relaxed -
- low - - rounded -

ɑ - Tongue is - high- and lips are - relaxed -
- low - - rounded -

o - Tongue is - high- and lips are - relaxed -
- low - - rounded -

u - Tongue is - high- and lips are - relaxed -
- low - - rounded -

3. Write a word in the blank provided that uses the given IPA sound. Don't use any of the words from above or on the previous page!

i ________________ ɑ ________________ u ________________

ɛ ________________ o ________________

Lesson 10: Sight-Singing

In order to learn a song, singers learn to read both rhythmic patterns and notes (melody) on the staff. Singing a melody for the first time is called "sight-singing." Below are some rhythmic examples using the notes introduced so far.

Hint: When singing rhythmic examples, take a breath on the rests: then you won't miss them! *Tap* and *say* the beats, then sing the examples on a La (choose any pitch that suits your voice).

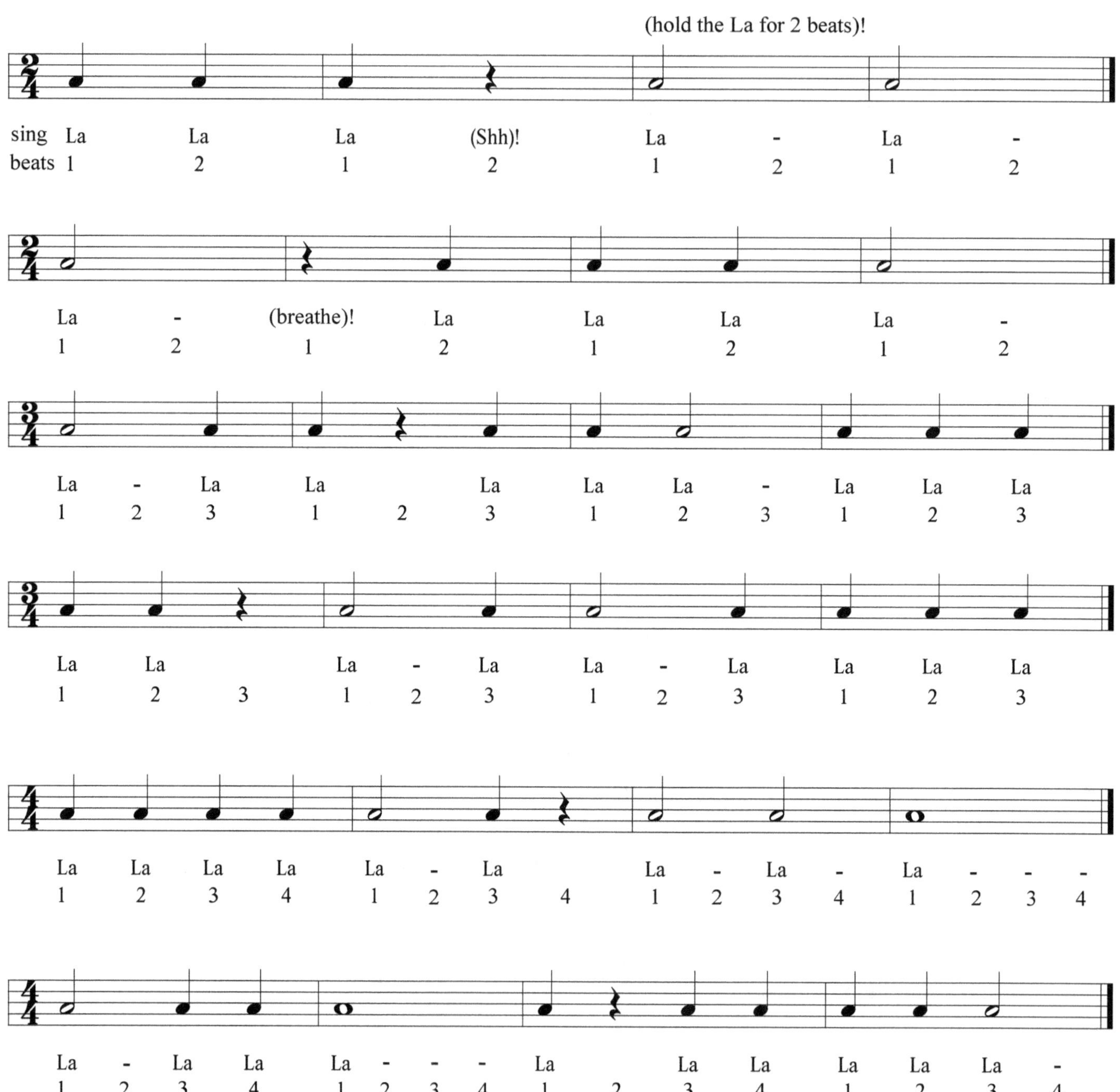

Melody & Solfege

Solfege is a system of assigning a syllable to each note of a scale, just like in the song "Do-Re-Mi" from the musical *The Sound of Music*.

Solfege is a useful tool when sight-singing. Moveable "Do" is when "Do" matches the **root** of whatever key you're in. The following examples contain a Major scale in the four keys covered in this level so far.

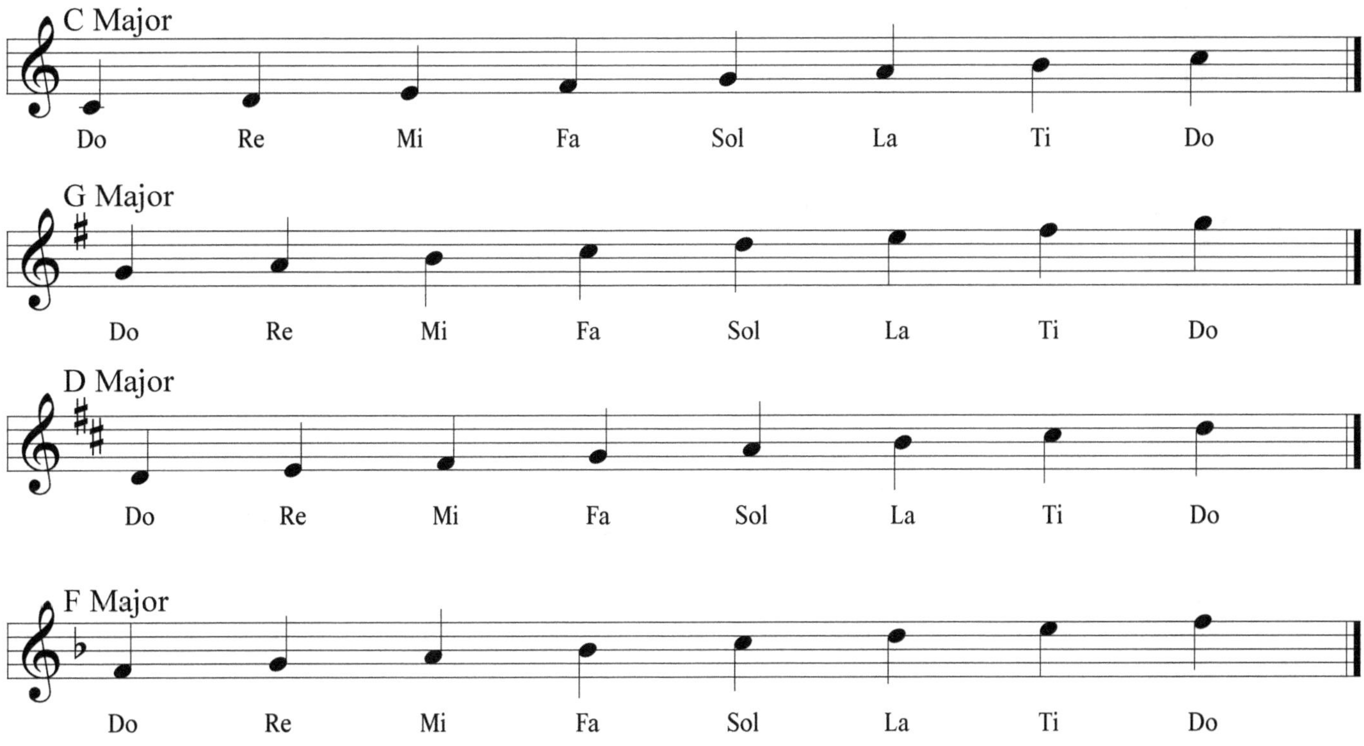

First you'll learn to sing melodies with Do, Re, Mi. The following melodies have the solfege written under the notes for you. Pay attention to the key signature changes. Use the picture of the piano below to find your starting note on your piano or piano app.

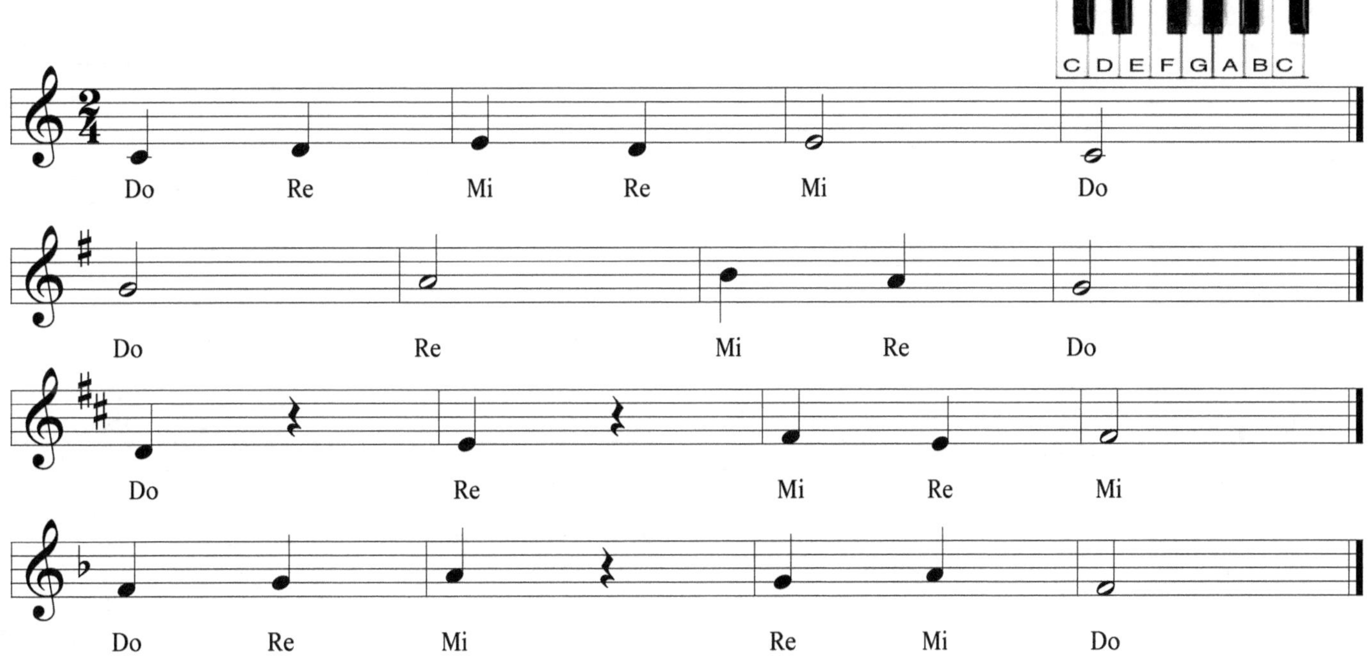

Review: Lesson 10

1. For the following melodies, write the note names, solfege & beats underneath the notes. Practice singing the examples when you are done!

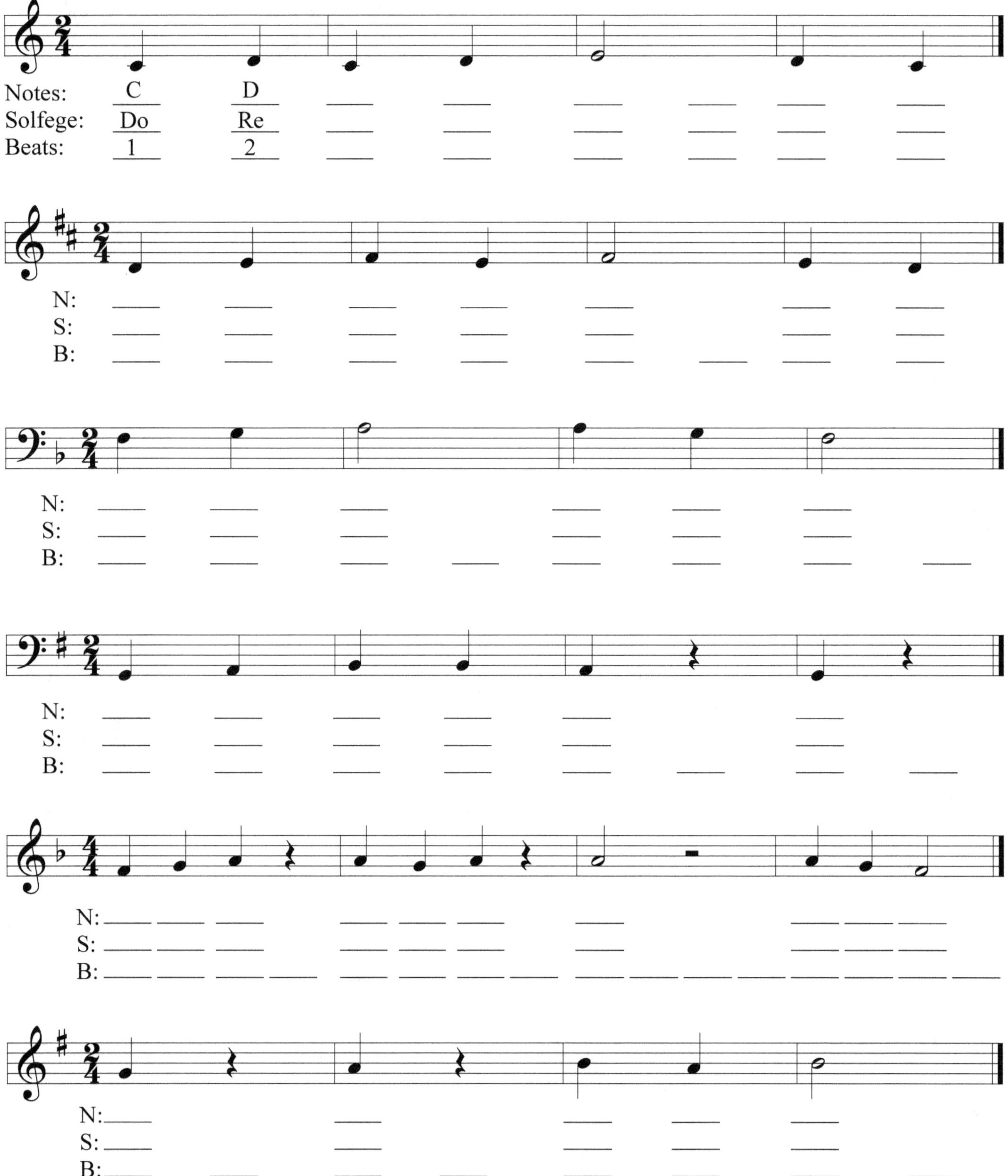

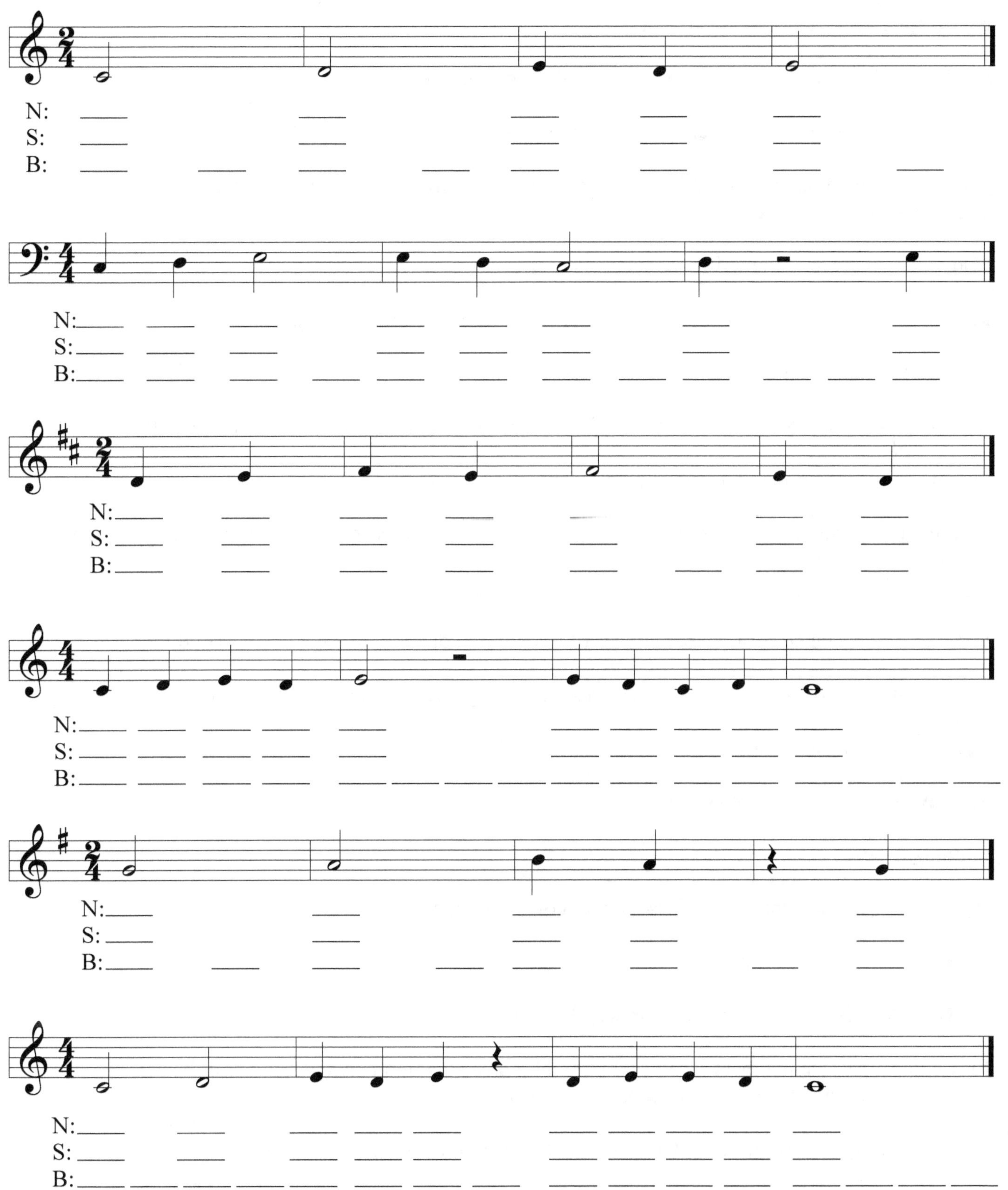
N:
S:
B:
N:
S:
B:
N:
S:
B:
N:
S:
B:
N:
S:
B:
N:
S:
B:

Lesson 11: Musical Terms

A crucial part of understanding music is being able to recognize and define musical terms. Below is a list of terms covered in this level with some additional ones.

accent (>) - to emphasize or stress a note

bar line - a line that separates notes on the staff into measures

bass clef (𝄢) - also called F clef, it names the fourth line of the bass staff

chord- more than one note sounding at the same time. A "triad" is a specific form of chord with 3 notes: a bottom note and the 3rd and 5th above it.

composer - a person who writes music

double bar line - two lines on a staff that indicate the end of a section or piece

fermata (𝄐) - a hold or pause

key signature - sharps or flats written on the staff at the beginning of a piece to indicate the key

flat (♭) - lowers the pitch of a note one-half step

folk music - music that is learned by mouth, has no known composer and was not initially written down

forte (*f*) - loud

interval - the distance between the pitches of two notes, sounded together or consecutively

IPA- the International Phonetic Alphabet: a standard representation of the sounds of spoken language

legato - smooth and connected

measure - the space between two bar lines

piano (*p*) - soft

sharp (#) - an accidental that raises the pitch of a note one-half step

staccato - short and detached

staff - the five lines and four spaces on which music is written

time signature - the numbers at the beginning of a piece that indicate the number of beats in each measure and the type of note that receives one beat

treble clef (𝄞) - also called G clef, it names the second line of the treble staff

vocalise - a vocal exercise

Review: Lesson 11

1. Check the appropriate answer for each of the following questions.

a. What divides music into measures?

____ bar line

____ measure

b. Which symbol raises the pitch of a note one-half step?

____ flat

____ sharp

c. What indicates a hold or pause in music?

____ interval

____ fermata

d. What is the name for sharps or flats written at the beginning of a piece that indicates the key?

____ time signature

____ key signature

e. What term means smooth and connected?

____ legato

____ staccato

f. What is another name for the F clef?

____ treble clef

____ bass clef

g. What is the symbol that means to sing softly?

____ forte

____ piano

h. Which key has 2 sharps in its key signature?

____ D Major

____ G Major

i. What word has the sound of the IPA symbol "ɛ"?

____ greed

____ fed

j. What is the name of the 5 lines and 4 spaces that music is written on?

____ bar line

____ staff

2. Complete the following crossword puzzle using the terms from this level.

Level 1 Crossword

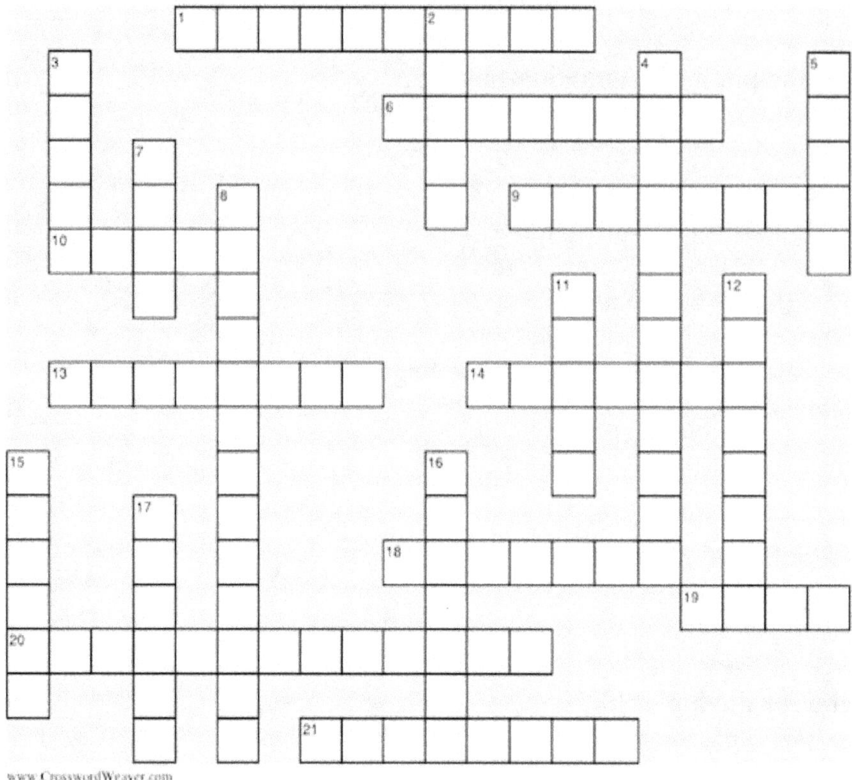

ACROSS

1 also called G clef, it names the second line of the treble staff (two words)
6 a person who writes music
9 also called F clef, it names the fourth line of the bass staff (two words)
10 soft
13 a vocal exercise
14 a hold or pause
18 a line that separates notes on the staff into measures (two words)
19 music that is learned by mouth, has no known composer, and was not initially written down
20 the numbers at the beginning of a piece that indicate the number of beats in each measure and the type of note that receives one beat (two words)
21 the distance between the pitches of two notes, sounded together or consecutively

DOWN

2 a group of 3 or more notes sounded at the same time
3 an accidental that raises the pitch of a note one-half step
4 sharps or flats written on the staff at the beginning of a piece to indicate the key
5 the five lines and four spaces on which music is written
7 lowers the pitch of a note one-half step
8 two lines on a staff that indicate the end of a section or piece (three words)
11 loud
12 short and detached
15 smooth and connected
16 the space between two bar lines
17 to emphasize or stress a note

crossword created at:
www.CrosswordWeaver.com

Lesson 12: Spotlight on Composers

An important part of music education is learning about the history of music. Studying composers allows for understanding the music we sing and why it was written the way it was. In this level you will learn about Alan Menken and Richard Rodgers.

ALAN MENKEN

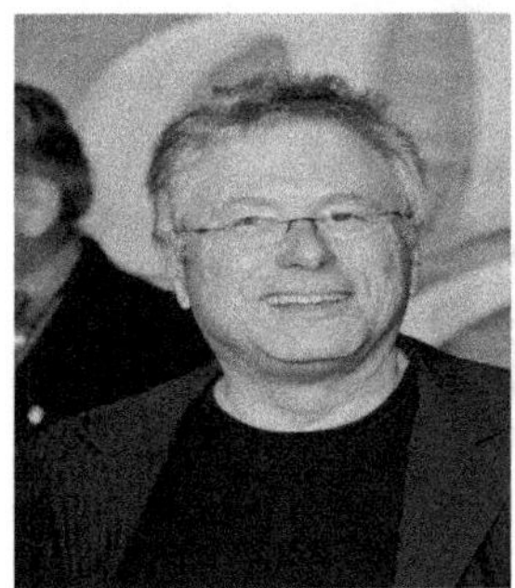

© Featureflash Photo Agency/Shutterstock.com

Alan Menken was born in the Contemporary period of music, on July 22nd, 1949 in Manhattan, NY.
When he was young he studied piano and violin. He went to college to study medicine, but soon changed his focus to music. After college, he composed music and also worked as an accompanist.

In 1982, Menken earned a Drama Desk Award nomination for his Off Broadway musical *Little Shop of Horrors.* This show became a successful motion picture and was later on Broadway.

Alan Menken is best known for his work with Walt Disney Pictures. He has written the scores for some of the most well known Disney movies including *The Little Mermaid, Aladdin, Beauty and the Beast, Pocahontas, The Hunchback of Notre Dame, Hercules,* and *Tangled.*

Both *Beauty and the Beast* and *The Little Mermaid* have become successful Broadway shows, and he has earned Tony Awards for each. So far, he has received 8 Oscars (Academy Awards) for his compositions for film, more wins than any other living person. He continues to compose music and resides in New York with his family.

Best Known Scores and Songs:

The Little Mermaid-*1989 (Movie), 2008 (Broadway Musical)*
"Under the Sea," "Part of Your World," "Kiss the Girl"
Beauty and the Beast-*1991 & 2017 (Movie), 1994 (Broadway Musical)*
"Be our Guest," "Belle," "Beauty and the Beast," "Gaston"
Aladdin-*1992 (Movie) 2014 (Broadway Musical)*
"A Whole New World," "A Friend Like Me," "Prince Ali" "Proud of Your boy"
Tangled-*2010 (Movie)*
"When will my Life Begin," "Mother Knows Best," "I've Got a Dream"
Hunchback of Notre Dame - *2014 (Broadway Musical)*
"Out There" "Topsy Turvy," "God Help the Outcasts"
Hercules- *1997 (Movie)*
"Go the Distance," "I Won't Say I'm in Love," "Zero to Hero"

RICHARD RODGERS

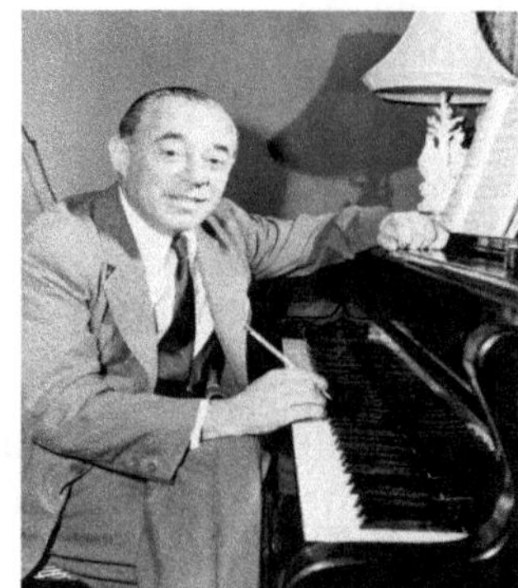

Bettmann/Contributor/Getty

Richard Rodgers was born in 1902 in the Contemporary Period of Music, in New York, NY. He studied music at both Columbia University and at Julliard.

For over 10 years, Rodgers collaborated with the lyricist Lorenz Hart. They wrote many successful musicals together including *Babes in Arms (1937)* and *Pal Joey (1940).* They also had hit songs including "Isn't it Romantic," "My Romance," and "My Funny Valentine."

Beginning in the early 1940's, Rodgers began working with lyricist Oscar Hammerstein. Their first hit musical which premiered in 1943 was *Oklahoma!* The next four musicals that Rodgers and Hammerstein wrote together are among the most popular musicals that also became movies. They are *Carousel, South Pacific, The King and I* and *The Sound of Music.* They also wrote the score to the film *State Fair* and a TV musical of *Cinderella.*

Rodgers and Hammerstein received 35 Tony Awards, 15 Academy Awards, two Pulitzer Prizes, two Grammy Awards, and two Emmy Awards for their musicals. Rodgers was the first person to win all four major awards, an EGOT (an Emmy, Grammy, Oscar and Tony) during the course of his career. He also won a Pulitzer Prize making him one of two people to receive all five awards.

Richard Rodgers married Dorothy Feiner in 1930. Their daughter, Mary, composed the musical *Once Upon a Mattress.* Their grandson, Adam Guettel won Tony Awards for Best Score and Orchestrations for *The Light in the Piazza* in 2005. Rodgers died in 1979, at the age of 77.

Best Known Scores and Songs:

The Sound of Music *(1959)*
"Do-Re-Mi," "Edelweiss," "My Favorite Things," "The Sound of Music"
Oklahoma! *(1943)*
"Oh, What a Beautiful Mornin,'" "People Will Say We're in Love," "Oklahoma!"
Carousel *(1945)*
"If I Loved You," "You'll Never Walk Alone," "June is Bustin' Out all Over"
The King and I *(1951)*
"I Whistle a Happy Tune," "Getting to Know you," "Shall We Dance"
South Pacific *(1949)*
"Dites-Moi," "Some Enchanted Evening," "I'm in Love with a Wonderful Guy"

Review: Lesson 12

1. Fill in the correct answer(s) to the following questions about Alan Menken & Richard Rodgers.

Alan Menken

a. Alan Menken was born in which country? ________________

b. He represents the ______________________ period of music.

c. He has won the ________ award at least 8 times.

d. What part of New York was he born in? ________________________

e. Some of the songs that Menken wrote from the movie __________________________ are "Be Our Guest," "Gaston," and "Belle."

f. He wrote the score for a Disney movie that also became a Broadway play in 2008. Name the movie: ______________________________

Richard Rodgers

a. Richard Rodgers was born in which country? ________________

b. He respresents the ______________________ period of music.

c. He wrote the musical *Oklahoma!* with the well known lyricist __________________________.

d. What is the name of the musical Rodgers wrote that contained the songs "Do-Re-Mi" and "My Favorite Things?" __________________________

e. He is one of the only people to have won four awards including the Emmy, Grammy, Oscar and

___________________.

f. What is the name of his grandson, who wrote the music for the musical *The Light in the Piazza?*

____

Level 1 Review Test

1. Look at the musical example below and fill in the appropriate letter next to the term. (8 points)

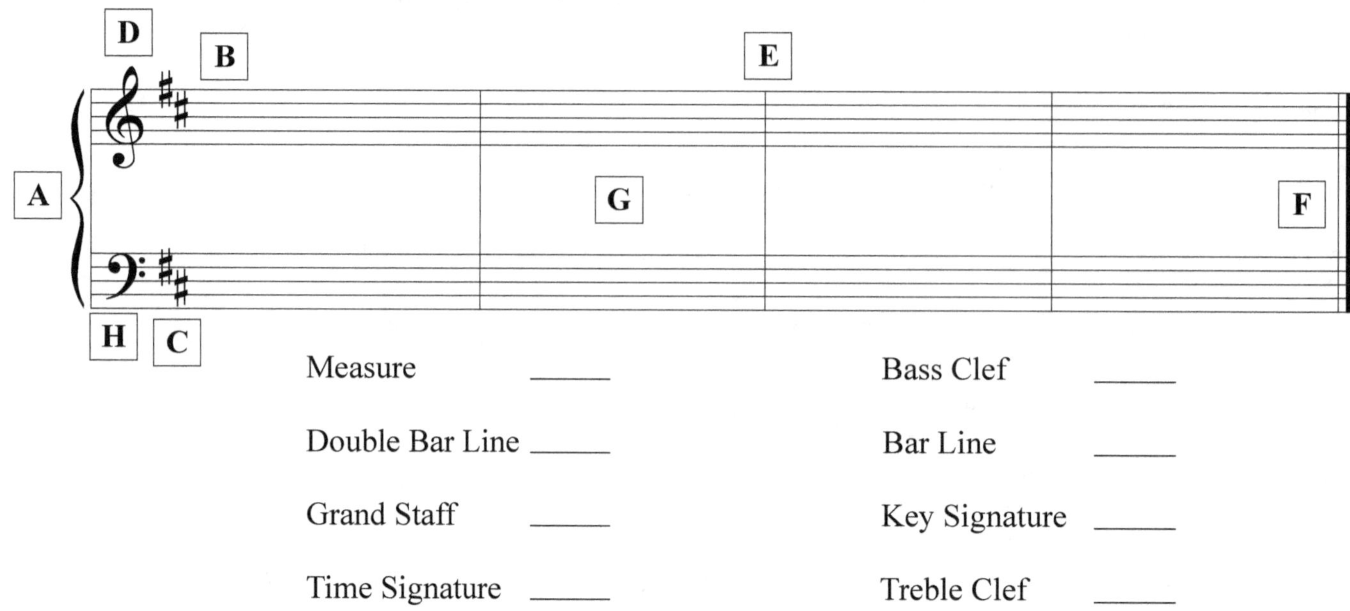

Measure	_____	Bass Clef	_____
Double Bar Line	_____	Bar Line	_____
Grand Staff	_____	Key Signature	_____
Time Signature	_____	Treble Clef	_____

2. Add correct stems to the notes below. (16 points-1 point for each correct stem)

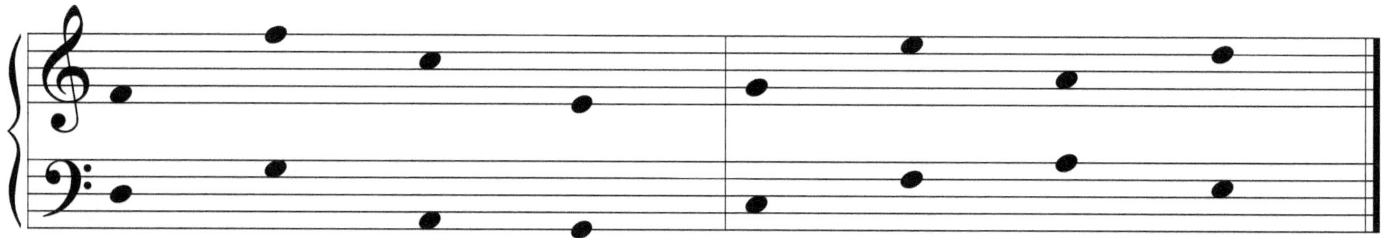

3. Write the letter names of the notes below. (20 points)

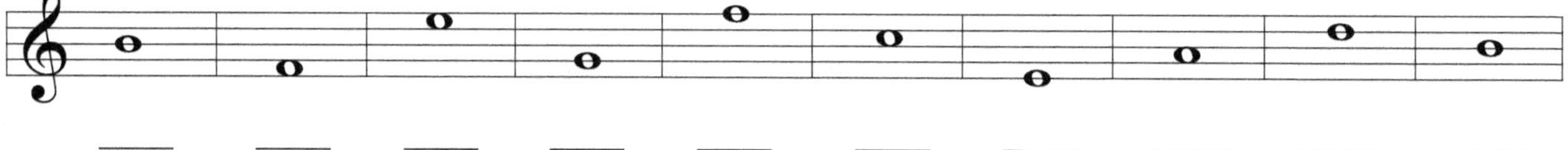

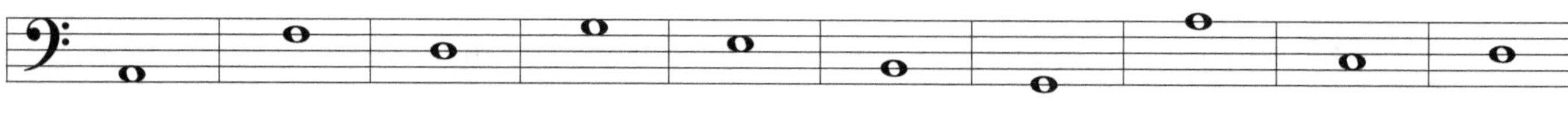

4. Name the following notes and their values *(for example: Quarter note, 1 beat)*. (12 points)

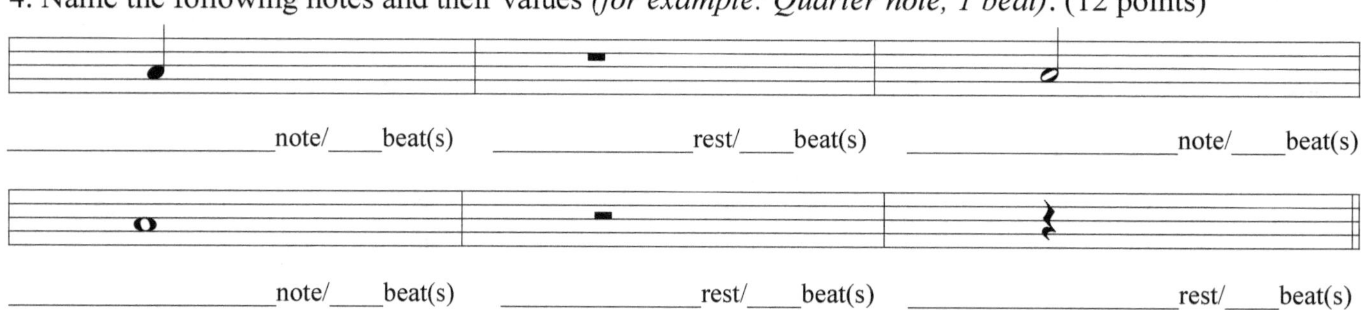

_______________note/____beat(s) _______________rest/____beat(s) _______________note/____beat(s)

_______________note/____beat(s) _______________rest/____beat(s) _______________rest/____beat(s)

5. Name the key signature and interval (2nd/3rd) for each example. (8 points)

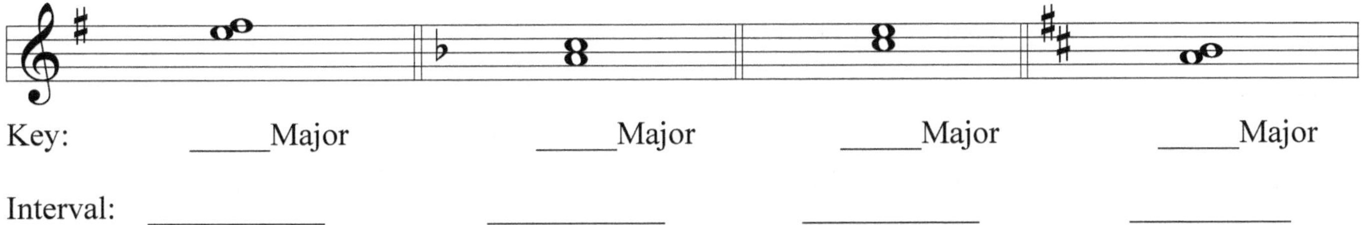

Key: _____Major _____Major _____Major _____Major

Interval: ___________ ___________ ___________ ___________

6. Each of these chords should have a Do (1), Mi (3), & Sol (5).
Fill in the missing note for each chord in both clefs to create a root position triad. (8 points)

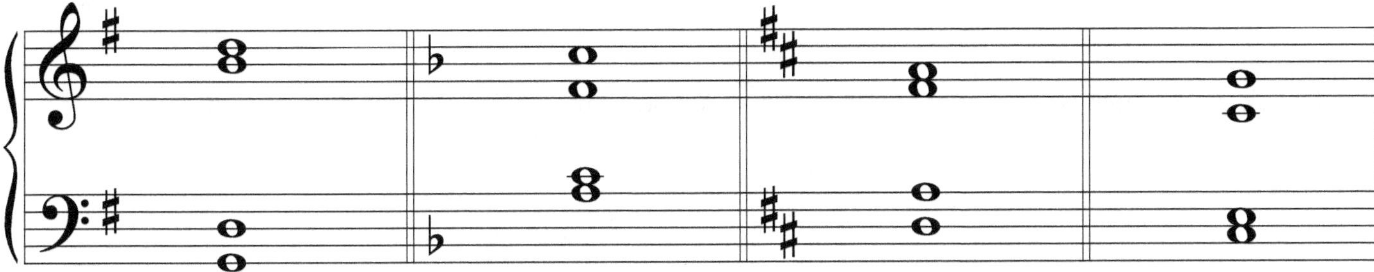

7. Write the beats under the examples. Pay attention to the time signatures!
(12 points- 1 point per correct measure)

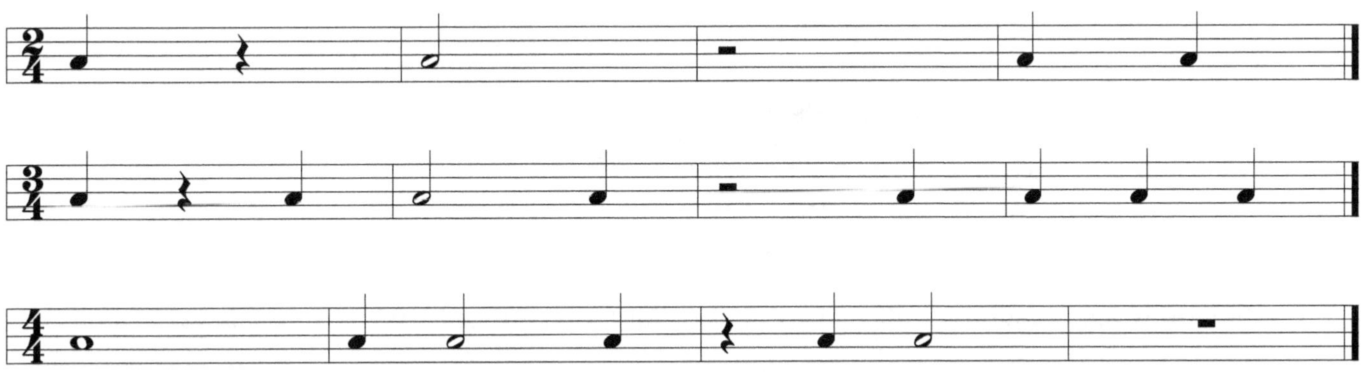

8. Write the note names and solfege under each note in the following examples. Don't forget to add ♯/♭ if needed. (12 points-1 point per correct measure: both solfege and notes must be correct)

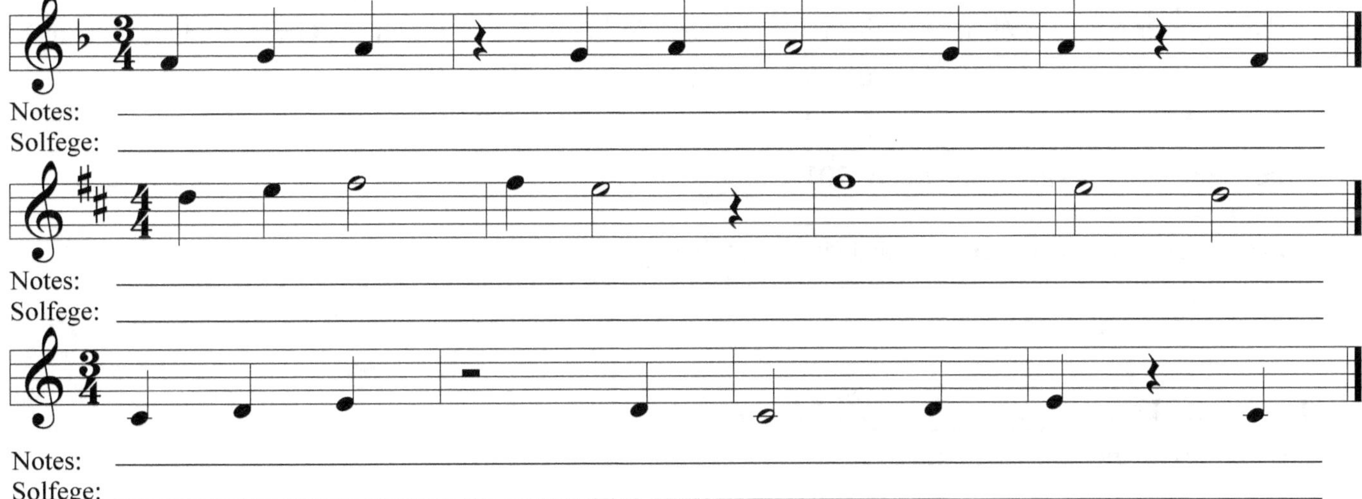

9. Fill in the correct answer using the musical terms in this level. (5 points)

a. An _________________ means to emphasize or stress a note.

b. The distance between two pitches is called an ________________.

c. The five lines and four spaces upon which music is written is called a ___________.

d. If the singing voice is smooth and connected it is ________________.

e. A ___________ is an accidental that raises a pitch by one half-step.

10. Check the English word that contains the same sound as the given IPA symbol. (5 points)

i ___White
___Keep

ɛ ___Best
___Leap

ɑ ___Pot
___Plate

o ___Goat
___Boot

u ___But
___Goose

11. For the following questions, write "Alan Menken" or "Richard Rodgers" as your answer. (5 points)

a. This composer wrote several scores for Disney musicals/movies. __________________________

b. This composer wrote the score for the musical/movie *The King and I.* __________________________

c. This composer has won all four major entertainment industry awards (Emmy, Grammy, Oscar, Tony).

____

d. Which composer is still living (as of 2017)? __________________________

e. Who worked with the lyricist Oscar Hammerstein? __________________________

Final Score:___________/111

answer key begins on the next page

Level 1 Review Test: Answers

1. Look at the musical example below and fill in the appropriate letter next to the term. (8 points)

1. Measure G
2. Double Bar Line F
3. Grand Staff A
4. Time Signature B
5. Bass Clef H
6. Bar Line E
7. Key Signature C
8. Treble Clef D

2. Add correct stems to the notes below. (16 points-1 point for each correct stem)

3. Write the letter names of the notes below. (20 points)

B F E G F C E A D B

A F D G E B G A C D

4. Name the following notes and their values *(for example: Quarter note, 1 beat)*. (12 points)

Quarter Note/1 beat　Whole Rest/4 beats　Half Note/2 beats

Whole Note/4 beats　Half Rest/2 beats　Quarter Rest/1 beat

5. Name the key signature and interval (2nd/3rd) for each example. (8 points)

G Major 2nd　F Major 3rd　C Major 3rd　D Major 2nd

6. Each of these chords should have a Do (1), Mi (3), & Sol (5).
Fill in the missing note for each chord in both clefs. (8 points)

7. Write the beats under the examples. Pay attention to the time signatures!
(12 points- 1 point per correct measure)

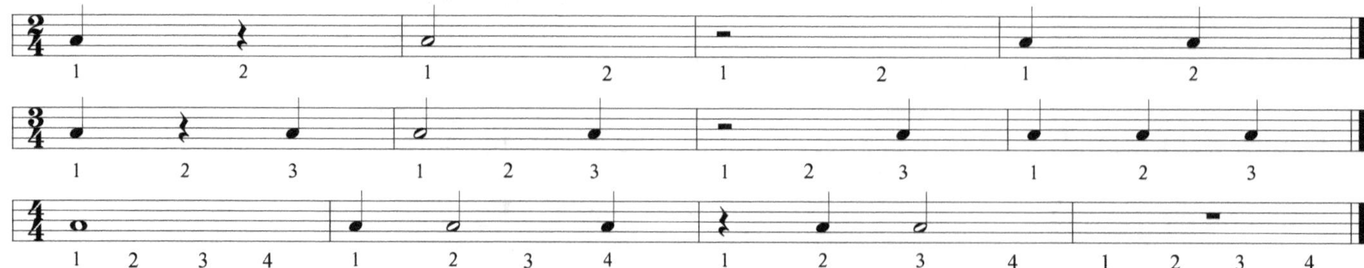

8. Write the note names and solfege under each note in the following examples.
(12 points-1 point per correct measure: both solfege and notes must be correct)

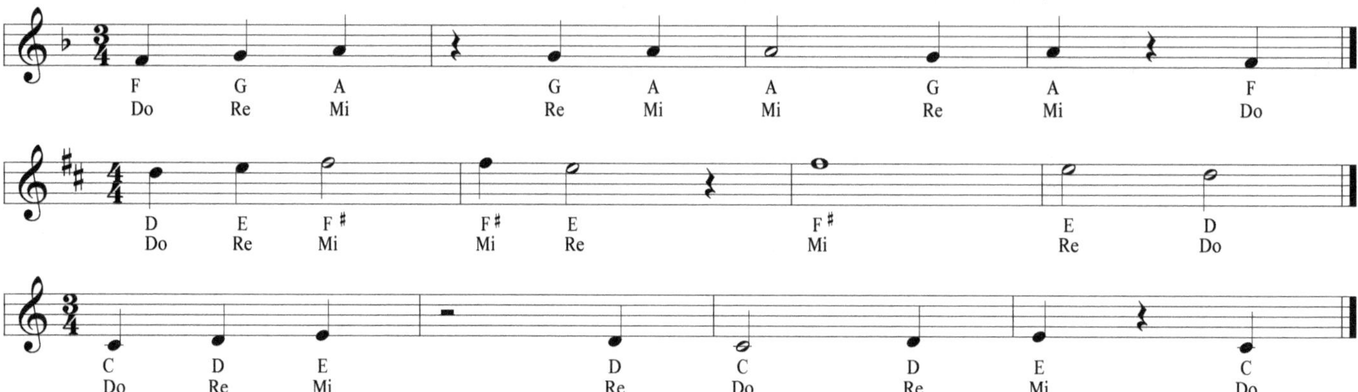

9. Fill in the correct answer using the musical terms in this level. (5 points)

a. accent b. interval c. staff d. legato e. staff

10. Check the English word that contains the same sound as the given IPA symbol. (5 points)

i - keep ɛ - best ɑ - pot o - goat u - goose

11. For the following questions, write "Alan Menken" or "Richard Rodgers" as your answer. (5 points)

a. Alan Menken

b. Richard Rodgers

c. Richard Rodgers

d. Alan Menken

e. Richard Rodgers

REFERENCES

Grout, Donald. *A History of Western Music.* New York, NY: W.W. Norton & Company, Inc., 1996.

Moriarty, John. *Diction*. Boston, MA: E. C. Schirmer Music Company, 1975.

Music Teachers' Association of California. *Certificate of Merit Voice Syllabus.* San Francisco: Music Teachers' Association of California, 2011.

Piston, Walter. *Harmony, Fifth Edition.* New York, NY: W.W. Norton & Company, Inc., 1987.

Plantinga, Leon. *Romantic Music, A History of Musical Style in Nineteenth-Century Europe.* New York, NY: W.W. Norton & Company, Inc., 1984.

Randel, Don Michael. *The Harvard Biographical Dictionary of Music.* Cambridge, Massachusetts: The Belknap Press of Harvard University Press, 1996.

Randel, Don Michael. *Harvard Concise Dictionary of Music.* Cambridge, Massachusetts: The Belknap Press of Harvard University Press, 1978.

Rushton, Julian. *Classical Music, A Concise History from Gluck to Beethoven.* London, England: Thames and Hudson Ltd., 1986.

The New Grove Dictionary of Music and Musicians. http://www.oxfordmusiconline.com., 2011

www.ingramcontent.com/pod-product-compliance
Lightning Source LLC
LaVergne TN
LVHW061257100826
845148LV00008B/1161